REMOTE WORK:
THE ULTIMATE GUIDE TO
FINDING LEGITIMATE
WORK-FROM-HOME JOBS

BY
HENRY E. PARKINS

COPYRIGHT PAGE

TABLE OF CONTENTS

INTRODUCTION

In recent years, the landscape of work has undergone a profound transformation. The traditional 9-to-5 office setup is no longer the sole paradigm of employment. Instead, a growing number of individuals are embracing remote work as a viable and attractive alternative. This shift has been accelerated by technological advancements, changing attitudes towards work-life balance, and the rise of a globalized economy.

Welcome to "Remote Work: The Ultimate Guide to Finding Legitimate Work-From-Home Jobs." In this book, we embark on a journey through the exciting and rapidly evolving world of remote work, offering insights, strategies, and practical advice for anyone seeking legitimate opportunities to work from the comfort of their own home.

Remote work, once considered a niche arrangement, has now become mainstream. From freelancers and digital nomads to full-time employees of remote-first companies, millions of individuals around the world are leveraging technology to redefine the way they work. The benefits are manifold: increased flexibility, reduced commuting time, improved work-life balance, and access to a global talent pool, to name just a few.

However, with the proliferation of remote work opportunities comes a myriad of challenges and complexities. Navigating the vast landscape of remote job boards, identifying legitimate opportunities amidst a sea of scams, honing the skills required for remote success, and maintaining productivity and well-being in a virtual environment - these are just a few of the hurdles that aspiring remote workers may encounter.

This book is designed to serve as your comprehensive guide through these challenges and beyond. Whether you're a seasoned remote worker looking to enhance your skills or someone considering remote work for the first time, you'll find valuable insights and practical advice within these pages.

We'll begin by exploring the fundamental concepts of remote work, delving into its advantages, challenges, and the skills required for success. From there, we'll dive into the practical aspects of finding legitimate remote jobs, including strategies for researching opportunities, crafting compelling applications, and avoiding scams.

Definition of Remote Work

Remote work, also known as telecommuting or telework, refers to a mode of employment where individuals perform their job duties from a location outside of a traditional office setting, typically from their own home or another remote location. This arrangement allows employees to carry out their tasks and responsibilities using technology-mediated communication tools, such as email, video conferencing, and collaboration software, without the need for physical proximity to their coworkers or employer.

Remote work encompasses a wide range of arrangements, from fully remote positions where employees work exclusively from home to hybrid models that combine remote and on-site work. It offers employees greater flexibility in terms of scheduling and location, enabling them to better balance their professional and personal lives. Additionally, remote work can lead to increased productivity, reduced commuting time and expenses, and access to a global talent pool for employers.

Importance and Prevalence of Remote Work

Remote work has emerged as a pivotal force reshaping the modern workforce, driven by technological advancements, shifting societal norms, and evolving attitudes towards work-life balance. Its importance and prevalence are underscored by several key factors:

Flexibility and Work-Life Balance: Remote work offers employees the flexibility to design their workday around their personal lives, allowing for a more harmonious balance between professional responsibilities and personal pursuits. This flexibility is especially valuable for individuals with caregiving responsibilities, health concerns, or other commitments that may make traditional office hours challenging.

Access to Talent and Global Markets: For employers, remote work expands the talent pool beyond geographic boundaries, enabling access to skilled professionals from diverse backgrounds and locations. By embracing remote work, companies can tap into a global talent market, fostering innovation, diversity, and competitiveness.

Cost Savings and Efficiency:
Remote work can yield significant cost savings for both employers and employees. Companies can reduce overhead expenses associated with office space, utilities, and infrastructure, while employees save on commuting costs, transportation time, and work-related expenses. Moreover, remote work has the potential to increase productivity and efficiency by minimizing distractions and optimizing work environments.

Environmental Impact:
By reducing the need for daily commutes and office facilities, remote work contributes to environmental sustainability by lowering carbon emissions, alleviating traffic congestion, and conserving natural resources. As organizations adopt remote work practices, they play a role in mitigating climate change and promoting eco-friendly alternatives to traditional work arrangements.

11

Adaptability and Resilience: The COVID-19 pandemic highlighted the importance of remote work as a means of maintaining business continuity in the face of unexpected disruptions. Organizations that had already embraced remote work were better equipped to navigate the challenges posed by the pandemic, demonstrating the resilience and adaptability inherent in remote work arrangements.

Workforce Diversity and Inclusion: Remote work has the potential to foster greater diversity and inclusion within organizations by removing barriers related to geographic location, mobility constraints, and physical accessibility. By embracing remote work, companies can create more inclusive work environments that accommodate diverse needs and perspectives.

The prevalence of remote work has surged in recent years, with a growing number of companies adopting remote-friendly policies and offering remote work options to their employees. According to research conducted by Global Workplace Analytics, remote work has experienced a significant uptick, with approximately 56% of the U.S. workforce holding jobs that are compatible with remote work arrangements. Furthermore, surveys indicate that a substantial portion of employees express a preference for remote or hybrid work models even beyond the pandemic era.

Purpose and Scope of the Book

The purpose of "Remote Work: The Ultimate Guide to Finding Legitimate Work-From-Home Jobs" is to provide readers with comprehensive guidance and practical strategies for navigating the dynamic landscape of remote work. Whether you're a seasoned remote worker looking to enhance your skills or someone considering remote work for the first time, this book aims to equip you with the knowledge, tools, and resources needed to succeed in remote employment.

The scope of the book encompasses various aspects of remote work, including:`

Understanding Remote Work: We begin by defining remote work and exploring its advantages, challenges, and the skills required for success in a remote environment. Readers will gain insights into the fundamental concepts and principles underlying remote work arrangements.

Finding Legitimate Remote Jobs:

This section offers practical advice for researching legitimate remote job opportunities, identifying red flags and scams, and crafting compelling job applications. Whether you're searching for freelance gigs, remote positions with established companies, or opportunities on remote work platforms, this section provides guidance on navigating the job market effectively.

Navigating Remote Work Platforms: As remote work platforms

continue to proliferate, understanding how to leverage these platforms effectively is essential. We explore popular remote work platforms, offer tips for creating appealing profiles, and provide insights into platform etiquette and best practices.

Developing Remote Work Skills:

Remote work requires a unique set of skills to thrive in a virtual environment. This section covers essential skills such as time management, communication, self-motivation, and collaboration, offering practical strategies for honing these skills and maximizing productivity.

Maintaining Work-Life Balance:

Achieving a healthy work-life balance is crucial for remote workers. We offer guidance on setting boundaries, creating productive workspaces, managing stress, and avoiding burnout, helping readers maintain equilibrium in their personal and professional lives.

Overcoming Remote Work Challenges:

Remote work presents its own set of challenges, from feelings of isolation to technological issues and communication barriers. We address common challenges faced by remote workers and provide strategies for overcoming them, fostering resilience and adaptability in remote work environments.

Advancing Your Remote Career:

For those looking to grow and advance in their remote careers, this section offers guidance on seeking opportunities for professional development, building a

15

personal brand, and positioning oneself for success in the remote work landscape.

Success Stories and Case Studies: Throughout the book, readers will encounter real-life success stories and case studies showcasing the diverse experiences and achievements of remote workers. These stories serve as inspiration and motivation, illustrating the possibilities and potential of remote work.

CHAPTER 1

UNDERSTANDING REMOTE WORK

Remote work, also known as telecommuting or telework, has emerged as a transformative force in the modern workforce, redefining how individuals approach their careers and employers structure their operations. In this section, we delve into the fundamental concepts of remote work, exploring its advantages, challenges, and the essential skills required for success in a remote environment.

Advantages of Remote Work:

Flexibility: Remote work offers unparalleled flexibility, allowing individuals to design their workday around their personal lives. Whether it's avoiding rush hour traffic, attending family events, or pursuing hobbies, remote work empowers employees to achieve a better balance between their professional and personal commitments.

17

Increased Productivity: Contrary to conventional wisdom, remote work has been shown to boost productivity for many individuals. Freed from the distractions of the office environment, remote workers often enjoy greater focus and efficiency, leading to improved performance and output.

Cost Savings: Remote work can yield significant cost savings for both employees and employers. From reduced commuting expenses and transportation costs to lower overhead for companies in terms of office space and utilities, remote work offers financial benefits that resonate with individuals and organizations alike.

Access to Global Talent: By embracing remote work, companies can tap into a vast pool of talent from around the world. Remote work transcends geographic boundaries, enabling organizations to recruit skilled professionals regardless of their location, fostering diversity, innovation, and competitiveness.

Environmental Sustainability: Remote work contributes to environmental sustainability by reducing carbon

18

emissions, alleviating traffic congestion, and conserving natural resources associated with daily commutes and office facilities. As organizations adopt remote work practices, they play a role in mitigating climate change and promoting eco-friendly alternatives to traditional work arrangements.

Challenges of Remote Work:

Isolation and Loneliness: Remote work can sometimes lead to feelings of isolation and loneliness, particularly for individuals accustomed to the social interactions of the traditional office environment. Maintaining connections with colleagues and establishing a support network are essential for combating these challenges.

Communication Barriers: Effective communication is critical in remote work environments, where face-to-face interactions are limited. Misunderstandings can arise due to differences in communication styles, time zones, or technological issues. Developing strong communication skills and leveraging appropriate tools and platforms are key to overcoming these barriers.

Work-Life Balance: While remote work offers flexibility, it can also blur the boundaries between work and personal life, leading to challenges in achieving a healthy balance. Setting clear boundaries, establishing routines, and prioritizing self-care are essential for maintaining equilibrium and preventing burnout.

Technological Challenges: Dependence on technology is inherent in remote work, making individuals vulnerable to technical glitches, connectivity issues, and cybersecurity threats. Staying informed about best practices for digital security, troubleshooting common technical problems, and being adaptable in the face of technological changes are essential for remote workers.

Distractions and Time Management: Without the structure of the traditional office environment, remote workers may struggle with distractions and time management. Establishing a dedicated workspace, setting realistic goals, and implementing effective time management strategies are crucial for maintaining focus and productivity.

Essential Skills for Remote Work Success:

Time Management: Remote work requires strong time management skills to prioritize tasks, set deadlines, and maintain productivity. Techniques such as time blocking, setting SMART goals, and minimizing distractions are essential for effective time management in a remote environment.

Communication: Clear and effective communication is paramount in remote work settings, where face-to-face interactions are limited. Remote workers must be proficient in written and verbal communication, actively seek clarification when needed, and leverage communication tools such as email, chat, and video conferencing to collaborate effectively with colleagues.

Self-Motivation: Remote work demands a high level of self-motivation and accountability. Without the external structure of the traditional office environment, remote workers must be proactive in setting goals, managing their workload, and staying focused on tasks.

Adaptability: **Flexibility and adaptability are essential qualities for success in remote work environments, which are characterized by constant change and uncertainty. Remote workers must be able to adapt to new technologies, workflows, and communication norms, embracing change as an opportunity for growth and innovation.**

Collaboration: **Collaboration is a cornerstone of remote work, requiring individuals to work effectively with colleagues across geographical distances and time zones. Remote workers must be skilled in collaborating virtually, fostering teamwork, and building strong relationships with colleagues despite physical separation.**

Advantages and Benefits of Remote Work

Remote work, also known as telecommuting or telework, offers a multitude of advantages and benefits for both employees and employers. In this section, we'll explore some of the key benefits of remote work and why it has become an increasingly attractive option

for individuals seeking flexibility, autonomy, and work-life balance.

Flexibility: One of the most significant advantages of remote work is the flexibility it offers. Remote workers have the freedom to set their own schedules, allowing them to work when they are most productive and accommodate personal commitments, such as childcare, appointments, or hobbies. This flexibility empowers individuals to achieve a better balance between their professional and personal lives, leading to greater satisfaction and well-being.

Reduced Commuting Stress: Remote work eliminates the need for daily commutes to and from the office, which can be stressful and time-consuming. By working from home or another remote location, employees can reclaim valuable time that would otherwise be spent stuck in traffic or navigating public transportation. This reduction in commuting stress can lead to improved mental health, increased productivity, and a better overall quality of life.

Cost Savings: Remote work can result in significant cost savings for both employees and employers. Remote workers save money on transportation expenses, such as gas, parking, or public transit fares, as well as work-related costs, such as meals, professional attire, and childcare. Employers can also save money by reducing overhead costs associated with maintaining office space, utilities, and equipment.

Increased Productivity: Contrary to common misconceptions, remote work has been shown to increase productivity for many individuals. Freed from the distractions of the office environment, remote workers often enjoy greater focus, autonomy, and efficiency. With the ability to customize their workspaces and schedules to suit their preferences, remote workers can optimize their environment for maximum productivity, resulting in higher-quality work and faster task completion.

Access to a Global Talent Pool: Remote work transcends geographic boundaries, allowing companies to access a diverse pool of talent from around the world. By embracing remote work, employers can recruit skilled professionals regardless of their location, fostering innovation, creativity, and diversity within their organizations. Remote work also enables companies to tap into specialized expertise that may not be available locally, leading to better outcomes and competitive advantage.

Better Work-Life Balance: Remote work enables individuals to achieve a better balance between their professional and personal lives, leading to improved overall well-being. With the flexibility to work from home or another remote location, employees can spend more time with their families, pursue personal interests, and engage in leisure activities without sacrificing their careers. This balance is essential for preventing burnout, reducing stress, and fostering long-term satisfaction and success.

Environmental Sustainability: Remote work has positive environmental impacts by reducing carbon emissions, traffic congestion, and energy consumption associated with daily commutes and office facilities. By eliminating the need for employees to travel to and from the office, remote work helps mitigate climate change, conserve natural resources, and promote sustainable living practices. As organizations adopt remote work policies, they contribute to a greener, more eco-friendly future for generations to come.

Challenges and Misconceptions of Remote Work

While remote work offers numerous advantages and benefits, it also comes with its own set of challenges and misconceptions that individuals may encounter. In this section, we'll explore some of the common challenges and misconceptions associated with remote work, and provide insights on how to address them effectively.

Isolation and Loneliness: One of the most significant challenges of remote work is the potential for isolation and loneliness. Working from home or another remote location can lead to feelings of social isolation, especially for individuals who are accustomed to the camaraderie and social interactions of the traditional office environment. Without the daily interactions with coworkers, remote workers may feel disconnected and lonely, which can impact their mental health and well-being.

Communication Barriers: Effective communication is essential for remote work success, but it can also be a significant challenge. Without the benefit of face-to-face interactions, remote workers must rely on digital communication tools such as email, chat, and video conferencing to collaborate with colleagues and communicate with their supervisors. Misunderstandings can arise due to differences in communication styles, time zones, or technological issues, leading to inefficiencies and conflicts within remote teams.

Work-Life Balance: While remote work offers flexibility, it can also blur the boundaries between work and personal life. Without the structure of the traditional office environment, remote workers may find it challenging to disconnect from work and establish a healthy work-life balance. The convenience of working from home can lead to longer work hours, difficulty unplugging after work, and feelings of burnout if not managed effectively.

Technological Challenges: Remote work relies heavily on technology, making individuals vulnerable to technical glitches, connectivity issues, and cybersecurity threats. Poor internet connections, malfunctioning software, and cyberattacks can disrupt workflow and compromise sensitive data, posing challenges for remote workers and their employers. Staying informed about best practices for digital security, troubleshooting common technical problems, and being adaptable in the face of technological changes are essential for remote work success.

Distractions and Time Management: Without the structure of the traditional office environment, remote workers may struggle with distractions and time management. Working from home can present numerous distractions, such as household chores, family members, or pets, that can interfere with productivity. Additionally, without a clear schedule and routine, remote workers may find it challenging to prioritize tasks and manage their time effectively.

Lack of Visibility and Recognition: Remote workers may face challenges in terms of visibility and recognition within their organizations. Without the physical presence in the office, remote workers may feel overlooked or undervalued, leading to feelings of disengagement and demotivation. Employers may also struggle to assess the performance and contributions of remote workers accurately, leading to potential biases and inequities in opportunities for advancement and recognition.

Misconceptions of Remote Work:

Remote Workers are Less Productive: One common misconception about remote work is that remote workers are less productive than their office-bound counterparts. However, numerous studies have shown that remote workers often report higher levels of productivity and job satisfaction due to the flexibility and autonomy afforded by remote work arrangements.

Remote Work is Only Suitable for Certain Jobs: Another misconception is that remote work is only suitable for certain types of jobs, such as IT or creative professions. In reality, remote work can be adapted to a wide range of industries and job roles, from customer service and administrative tasks to project management and marketing.

Remote Work is Isolating and Lonely: While remote work can be isolating for some individuals, it's not inherently lonely. With the right strategies and support systems in place, remote workers can maintain connections with colleagues, build virtual communities, and foster a sense of belonging within their organizations.

Remote Work is Temporary: In the wake of the COVID-19 pandemic, there is a misconception that remote work is merely a temporary measure until things return to "normal." However, remote work was on the rise long before the pandemic, and many companies are embracing remote work as a permanent or long-term strategy to attract and retain top talent, reduce costs, and promote flexibility.

30

Skills and Traits Required for Successful Remote Work

Remote work presents unique challenges and opportunities that require a specific set of skills and traits for individuals to thrive in a virtual environment. In this section, we'll explore some of the key skills and traits that are essential for successful remote work:

Self-Motivation: Remote work requires a high level of self-motivation and initiative. Without the structure and supervision of the traditional office environment, remote workers must be proactive in setting goals, managing their workload, and staying focused on tasks. Self-motivated individuals are able to stay on track, meet deadlines, and achieve their objectives even when working independently.

Time Management: Effective time management is crucial for remote work success. Remote workers must be able to prioritize tasks, set deadlines, and allocate their time efficiently to meet project requirements and deadlines. Techniques such as time blocking, setting SMART goals, and minimizing distractions are

31

essential for maximizing productivity and managing workload effectively.

Communication Skills: Clear and effective communication is paramount in remote work environments, where face-to-face interactions are limited. Remote workers must be proficient in written and verbal communication, able to articulate their ideas clearly, and convey information accurately to colleagues and clients. Strong communication skills facilitate collaboration, foster teamwork, and build rapport with remote teammates.

Adaptability: Flexibility and adaptability are essential qualities for success in remote work environments, which are characterized by constant change and uncertainty. Remote workers must be able to adapt to new technologies, workflows, and communication norms, embracing change as an opportunity for growth and innovation. Adaptable individuals are resilient in the face of challenges and able to thrive in dynamic work environments.

Problem-Solving Skills: Remote work often presents unique challenges and

32

obstacles that require creative problem-solving skills to overcome. Whether troubleshooting technical issues, resolving conflicts with colleagues, or navigating complex projects, remote workers must be adept at identifying solutions and implementing effective strategies to address problems as they arise. Problem-solving skills enable remote workers to overcome obstacles and achieve their goals with confidence.

Organizational Skills: Strong organizational skills are essential for remote work success, as remote workers must manage their time, tasks, and resources effectively to stay productive and focused. Remote workers must be able to prioritize tasks, set deadlines, and maintain a structured workflow to meet project requirements and expectations. Organizational skills enable remote workers to stay on top of their workload, manage competing priorities, and deliver high-quality work consistently.

Independence and Accountability: Remote work requires a degree of independence and

accountability, as remote workers are responsible for managing their own time and workload. Remote workers must be able to work autonomously, make decisions independently, and take ownership of their work and outcomes. Individuals who demonstrate independence and accountability are reliable, trustworthy, and capable of delivering results with minimal supervision.

Collaboration and Teamwork:

Collaboration is a cornerstone of remote work, requiring individuals to work effectively with colleagues across geographical distances and time zones. Remote workers must be skilled in collaborating virtually, leveraging communication tools and technologies to coordinate tasks, share information, and solve problems collaboratively. Strong teamwork skills enable remote workers to build relationships, foster camaraderie, and achieve common goals as part of a remote team.

CHAPTER 2

FINDING LEGITIMATE REMOTE JOBS

In today's digital age, the internet has become a valuable resource for finding legitimate remote job opportunities. However, amidst the plethora of online job boards and platforms, identifying legitimate remote jobs can be a daunting task. In this section, we'll explore practical strategies for finding legitimate remote jobs and avoiding scams:

Research Legitimate Remote Job Boards and Platforms: **Start your search by exploring reputable remote job boards and platforms that specialize in remote work opportunities. Websites such as FlexJobs, Remote.co, We Work Remotely, and Remote OK curate legitimate remote job listings from reputable companies across various industries. These platforms often feature remote jobs from well-established companies that have a track record of offering remote work options to their employees.**

Check Company Websites: In addition to remote job boards, consider visiting the websites of companies you're interested in working for to explore remote job opportunities directly. Many companies, including large corporations and startups, post remote job listings on their career pages or dedicated remote work sections. By checking company websites, you can discover remote job openings that may not be advertised elsewhere and gain insights into the company culture and remote work policies.

Network and Referrals: Networking remains a powerful tool for finding remote job opportunities, even in the digital age. Leverage your professional network, including colleagues, friends, and former classmates, to inquire about remote job openings or referrals to remote-friendly companies. Join online communities and forums dedicated to remote work, such as LinkedIn groups or Reddit communities, where you can connect with fellow remote workers, share job leads, and exchange insights and advice.

Use Specific Keywords in Your Search: When searching for remote jobs online, use specific keywords related to remote work, such as "remote," "telecommute," "work from home," or "virtual." Including these keywords in your search queries will help narrow down job listings to remote opportunities specifically. Additionally, consider using industry-specific keywords relevant to your skills and experience to refine your search further.

Beware of Red Flags and Scams: While searching for remote jobs online, it's essential to be vigilant and watch out for red flags that may indicate potential scams. Beware of job listings that promise unrealistic earnings, require upfront payments or investments, or lack detailed information about the company or job responsibilities. Research companies and employers thoroughly, check for reviews and ratings, and trust your instincts if something seems too good to be true.

Verify Job Listings and Employers: Before applying to remote job listings, take the time to verify the legitimacy of the job and the employer. Look for contact information, such as a company website, email address, or phone number, to reach out and inquire about the job posting directly. Research the company's reputation, reviews, and presence on social media and professional networking sites to ensure they are reputable and trustworthy.

Protect Your Personal Information: When applying for remote jobs online, exercise caution when sharing personal information, such as your social security number, banking details, or other sensitive information. Legitimate employers will not ask for sensitive information upfront during the application process. Use secure and reputable platforms for job applications, and be wary of any requests for payment or personal information before you've been hired.

Researching Legitimate Remote Job Opportunities

Finding legitimate remote job opportunities requires careful research and diligence to ensure that you are applying for positions that align with your skills, experience, and career goals. In this section, we'll explore practical strategies for researching legitimate remote job opportunities:

Utilize Online Job Boards and Platforms: There are numerous online job boards and platforms dedicated to remote work opportunities. Websites such as Remote.co, FlexJobs, We Work Remotely, and RemoteOK specialize in listing legitimate remote job openings across various industries and job roles. These platforms allow you to filter job listings based on your preferences, such as job type, location, and industry, making it easier to find remote opportunities that match your qualifications and interests.

Explore Company Websites: Many companies offer remote work options for their employees and may advertise remote job openings directly on their websites. Take the time to explore the careers or job opportunities section of companies that interest you to see if they have remote positions available. Subscribe to their newsletters or follow them on social media to stay updated on new job openings and remote work opportunities.

Network and Referrals: Networking is a valuable tool for uncovering hidden remote job opportunities and gaining insights into companies that offer remote work options. Reach out to your professional network, including former colleagues, mentors, and industry contacts, to inquire about remote job openings or referrals. Attend industry events, conferences, and virtual meetups to expand your network and connect with professionals who may be able to offer insights or job leads.

Join Remote Work Communities:

Joining online communities and forums dedicated to remote work can provide valuable resources and networking opportunities. Websites such as Reddit's r/digitalnomad, LinkedIn Groups focused on remote work, and specialized forums like Nomad List or Digital Nomad Forum are great places to connect with like-minded individuals, share experiences, and discover remote job opportunities.

Research Remote-Friendly Companies:

Some companies have embraced remote work as part of their company culture and offer remote work options for their employees. Research companies that are known for their remote-friendly policies and company culture, such as fully remote companies, distributed teams, or companies with flexible work arrangements. Websites like Glassdoor, LinkedIn, and company review sites can provide insights into companies' remote work policies and employee experiences.

Attend Virtual Career Fairs and Events:
Virtual career fairs and events offer opportunities to connect with employers and recruiters who are actively hiring for remote positions. Look for virtual career fairs specifically focused on remote work or industries that commonly offer remote opportunities. Participate in networking sessions, attend informational webinars, and engage with recruiters to learn about remote job openings and showcase your skills and qualifications.

Set Up Job Alerts:
Many job boards and platforms offer the option to set up job alerts based on your preferences and criteria. Take advantage of this feature to receive notifications about new remote job openings that match your skills and interests. Customize your job alerts to receive notifications for specific keywords,

41

job types, or industries, ensuring that you stay informed about relevant remote job opportunities as soon as they become available.

By utilizing these strategies and resources for researching legitimate remote job opportunities, you can increase your chances of finding remote work that aligns with your skills, experience, and career aspirations. In the following sections of this book, we'll explore tips for crafting compelling job applications, identifying red flags and scams, and navigating the remote work landscape effectively.

Online Job Boards and Platforms for Remote Work Opportunities

When searching for legitimate remote work-from-home jobs, online job boards and platforms are invaluable resources that can connect you with a wide range of remote job opportunities across various industries and job roles. In this section, we'll explore some of the top online job boards and platforms dedicated to remote work:

FlexJobs: FlexJobs is a leading job board specializing in remote, freelance, and flexible job opportunities. Their curated database features thousands of remote job listings from reputable companies across the globe. FlexJobs thoroughly screens and verifies each job posting to ensure legitimacy, making it a trusted resource for remote job seekers.

Remote.co: Remote.co is a platform that offers a curated list of remote job opportunities from companies of all sizes and industries. Their job listings include full-time, part-time, and freelance remote positions, as well as remote-friendly companies that embrace distributed workforces. Remote.co also provides resources and insights for remote job seekers, including tips for navigating the remote job market and building remote-friendly skills.

We Work Remotely: We Work Remotely is one of the largest remote job boards, featuring remote job opportunities in fields such as programming, design, marketing, and customer support. Their job listings are updated regularly and cover a wide range of industries and job functions. We Work Remotely offers both full-time and contract remote positions, making it a versatile resource for remote job seekers.

RemoteOK: RemoteOK is a remote job board that aggregates remote job listings from various sources, including company websites, job boards, and social media. Their platform features remote job opportunities in tech, design, marketing, and other fields, with options for both full-time and freelance remote work. RemoteOK also allows users to filter job listings by location, job type, and keyword to find remote jobs that match their preferences.

Virtual Vocations: Virtual Vocations is a job board specializing in telecommuting and remote job opportunities. Their platform features remote job listings across a wide range of industries, including healthcare, education, sales, and administration. Virtual Vocations offers resources such as remote job search guides, resume writing tips, and career coaching services to support remote job seekers throughout their job search journey.

LinkedIn: LinkedIn is a professional networking platform that also serves as a valuable resource for finding remote job opportunities. Users can search for remote job listings using the platform's job search feature and filter results by location, job type, and industry. Additionally, LinkedIn allows users to follow companies that offer remote work options and join remote work-related groups and communities to connect with other remote professionals and stay updated on remote job openings.

RemoteHub: RemoteHub is a platform that aggregates remote job listings from various sources, including remote job boards, company websites, and social media. Their platform features remote job opportunities in tech, marketing, design, and other fields, with options for full-time, part-time, and freelance remote work. RemoteHub also provides resources and guides for remote job seekers, including tips for building a remote-friendly resume and preparing for remote job interviews.

Company Websites Offering Remote Work Opportunities

Exploring company websites directly can be an effective way to discover legitimate remote work opportunities. Many companies offer remote work options for their employees and advertise remote job openings on their websites. Here are some reputable companies known for offering remote work opportunities:

Automattic (WordPress):

Automattic, the company behind WordPress.com, is known for its distributed workforce and remote-friendly culture. They frequently hire for remote positions in areas such as engineering, customer support, marketing, and design. Job seekers can explore their careers page to find current remote job openings.

GitLab: GitLab is a fully remote company that provides a web-based DevOps platform for developers. They have a remote-first culture and offer a wide range of remote job opportunities in engineering, product management, marketing, sales, and more. Job seekers can visit their careers page to browse current remote job openings.

46

Zapier: Zapier is a remote company that offers a web-based automation tool that connects various apps and services. They have a distributed team of remote employees and frequently hire for remote positions in areas such as engineering, customer support, marketing, and product management. Job seekers can explore their careers page to find remote job opportunities.

InVision: InVision is a design collaboration platform that allows teams to create, prototype, and collaborate on digital designs. They have a remote-friendly culture and offer remote job opportunities in areas such as engineering, design, product management, sales, and customer support. Job seekers can visit their careers page to explore current remote job openings.

Buffer: Buffer is a social media management platform that helps businesses schedule and analyze their social media posts. They have a distributed team of remote employees and offer remote job opportunities in areas such as engineering, product management, marketing, and customer support. Job seekers can explore their careers page to find remote job openings.

Basecamp: Basecamp is a project management and team collaboration software company known for its remote-friendly culture. They have a distributed team of remote employees and frequently hire for remote positions in areas such as engineering, design, customer support, and marketing. Job seekers can visit their careers page to browse current remote job opportunities.

Toptal: Toptal is a talent marketplace that connects companies with top freelancers in fields such as software development, design, finance, and project management. They offer remote job opportunities for freelancers to work on projects with clients from around the world. Freelancers can apply to join Toptal's network and access remote job opportunities through their platform.

Networking and Referrals for Remote Work Opportunities

Networking and referrals can be powerful tools for uncovering hidden remote job opportunities and gaining insights into companies that offer remote work options. Building and leveraging your professional network can open doors to remote job opportunities that may not be advertised publicly. Here are some strategies for networking and leveraging referrals to find legitimate remote work-from-home jobs:

Reach Out to Your Existing Network: Start by reaching out to your existing network of colleagues, friends, family members, and acquaintances to let them know that you are seeking remote work opportunities. Share your skills, experience, and career goals with them, and ask if they know of any remote job openings or companies that offer remote work options. Personal connections can often provide valuable insights and referrals to remote job opportunities.

Attend Virtual Networking Events: Virtual networking events,

49

webinars, and conferences provide opportunities to connect with professionals in your industry and expand your network. Look for virtual events specifically focused on remote work or industries that commonly offer remote opportunities. Participate in networking sessions, engage with fellow attendees, and exchange contact information to build relationships and uncover remote job opportunities.

Join Remote Work Communities and Forums:

Joining online communities and forums dedicated to remote work can provide valuable resources, support, and networking opportunities. Websites such as Reddit's r/digitalnomad, LinkedIn Groups focused on remote work, and specialized forums like Nomad List or Digital Nomad Forum are great places to connect with like-minded individuals, share experiences, and discover remote job opportunities through networking.

Utilize LinkedIn:

LinkedIn is a powerful platform for professional networking and can be a valuable resource for uncovering remote job opportunities.

50

Connect with professionals in your industry, including recruiters, hiring managers, and remote work advocates. Join LinkedIn Groups and communities focused on remote work, and participate in discussions to network with other remote professionals and learn about remote job openings.

Engage with Remote-Friendly Companies: Research companies that are known for their remote-friendly policies and company culture. Follow these companies on social media, engage with their content, and connect with employees who work remotely. Express your interest in remote work opportunities and inquire about potential job openings or referrals. Building relationships with employees of remote-friendly companies can increase your chances of being referred for remote job opportunities.

Offer to Provide Value: When networking with professionals in your industry, offer to provide value in exchange for insights or referrals. Offer to share your expertise, provide feedback on projects, or help solve a problem they may be facing.

Building genuine relationships and offering value can increase the likelihood of receiving referrals for remote job opportunities from your network.

Express Your Interest in Remote Work:

Make it known to your network that you are actively seeking remote work opportunities. Update your LinkedIn profile and other professional profiles to indicate your interest in remote work and highlight your remote work skills and experience. Share articles, blog posts, or resources related to remote work to demonstrate your commitment and interest in remote employment.

Identifying Red Flags and Scams in Remote Work Opportunities

While remote work offers numerous benefits and opportunities, it's essential to be vigilant and cautious when evaluating job postings and opportunities to avoid falling victim to scams or fraudulent schemes. In this section, we'll explore some common red flags and scams to watch out for when searching for legitimate remote work-from-home jobs:

Unsolicited Job Offers: Be wary of unsolicited job offers that come out of the blue, especially if they promise high earnings with minimal effort or qualifications. Legitimate employers typically don't reach out to candidates directly without prior interaction or application.

Requests for Upfront Payment: Beware of job postings or opportunities that require you to pay upfront fees or expenses as a condition of employment. Legitimate employers do not ask job seekers to pay for job opportunities, training, equipment, or background checks.

Vague Job Descriptions: Pay attention to job postings with vague or ambiguous job descriptions, requirements, or responsibilities. Legitimate job postings should provide clear details about the job role, qualifications, responsibilities, and compensation.

Unprofessional Communication: Watch out for poor grammar, spelling

errors, or unprofessional communication in job postings, emails, or correspondence from potential employers. Legitimate employers typically maintain professional communication standards in their interactions with candidates.

Pressure to Act Quickly: Be cautious of job opportunities that pressure you to make quick decisions or take immediate action, such as signing contracts or providing personal information without adequate time for review or consideration.

Overly Generous Compensation Offers: Exercise caution if a job offer promises exceptionally high compensation or benefits that seem too good to be true. Scammers may use enticing compensation offers to lure unsuspecting job seekers into fraudulent schemes.

Requests for Personal Information: Be cautious of job postings or opportunities that request sensitive personal information upfront, such as your social security number, bank account details, or copies of identification documents. Legitimate employers typically collect this information later in the hiring process and through secure channels.

Lack of Company Information: Research the company offering the remote job opportunity and verify its legitimacy before applying or accepting any offers. Beware of job postings that lack company information, such as a company website, physical address, contact information, or online presence.

Unsolicited Requests for Payment Processing: Be wary of job opportunities that involve processing payments or financial transactions on behalf of the employer, especially if they ask you to use your personal bank account for receiving and forwarding payments. These roles may be part of fraudulent money laundering or payment processing scams.

Phishing Emails and Scam Websites: Be vigilant of phishing emails, fake job postings, or scam websites that mimic legitimate companies or job boards to steal personal information, credentials, or financial data. Verify the legitimacy of websites and email addresses before providing any sensitive information or clicking on links.

Tips for Crafting a Compelling Remote Job Application

Crafting a compelling remote job application is essential to stand out from the competition and increase your chances of securing remote work-from-home opportunities. Here are some tips to help you create a strong and compelling remote job application:

Tailor Your Resume and Cover Letter: Customize your resume and cover letter to highlight relevant skills, experiences, and achievements that align with the job requirements and responsibilities. Tailoring your application demonstrates your genuine interest in the position and showcases how your qualifications make you an ideal candidate for the role.

Highlight Remote Work Experience: Emphasize any previous remote work experience or relevant skills

that demonstrate your ability to thrive in a remote work environment. Highlight your experience with remote collaboration tools, time management skills, and self-motivation to showcase your readiness for remote work.

Demonstrate Remote-Friendly Skills:
Showcase skills that are essential for remote work success, such as strong communication skills, adaptability, problem-solving abilities, and proficiency with remote collaboration tools and technologies. Provide examples of how you have successfully utilized these skills in previous roles or projects.

Quantify Your Achievements:
Use quantifiable metrics and specific examples to demonstrate your accomplishments and contributions in previous roles. Highlighting measurable results, such as increased sales, improved efficiency, or cost savings, provides concrete evidence of your impact and value as an employee.

Address Remote-Specific Concerns:
Anticipate and address any concerns or questions that employers may

have about your ability to work remotely. Assure employers of your reliability, availability, and commitment to remote work by addressing potential concerns proactively in your application materials.

Showcase Your Tech Savvy:

Highlight your proficiency with remote work tools, software, and technologies commonly used in virtual work environments. Mention any relevant certifications, training, or experiences with remote collaboration tools, project management software, video conferencing platforms, and communication tools to demonstrate your tech-savvy skills.

Emphasize Your Self-Motivation and Autonomy:

Remote work requires self-motivation, initiative, and the ability to work independently without direct supervision. Showcase your ability to manage your time effectively, prioritize tasks, and stay focused on goals to demonstrate your readiness for remote work.

Provide References and Testimonials:

Include references or

testimonials from previous employers, colleagues, or clients who can vouch for your skills, work ethic, and reliability as a remote worker. Positive testimonials and endorsements can reinforce your qualifications and credibility as a candidate.

Follow Application Instructions Carefully:

Pay close attention to the application instructions provided by the employer and ensure that you follow them carefully. Submit all required materials, such as a resume, cover letter, portfolio, or writing samples, in the specified format and within the designated timeframe to demonstrate your attention to detail and professionalism.

Follow Up Appropriately:

After submitting your application, follow up with the employer appropriately to express your continued interest in the position and inquire about the status of your application. Send a polite and professional follow-up email or message, thanking the employer for considering your application and reiterating your enthusiasm for the opportunity.

CHAPTER 3

NAVIGATING REMOTE WORK PLATFORMS

Remote work platforms serve as valuable resources for individuals seeking legitimate work-from-home opportunities across various industries and job roles. Navigating these platforms effectively can help remote job seekers discover relevant job listings, connect with remote-friendly companies, and streamline the job application process. Here are some tips for navigating remote work platforms effectively:

Create a Detailed Profile: When signing up for a remote work platform, take the time to create a detailed profile that highlights your skills, experience, and qualifications relevant to remote work. Include keywords related to remote work, such as "telecommuting," "virtual," or "remote," to increase your visibility to employers searching for remote talent.

Set Up Job Alerts: Many remote work platforms offer the option to set up job alerts based on your preferences and criteria. Take advantage of this feature to receive notifications about new remote job openings that match your skills and interests. Customize your job alerts to receive notifications for specific keywords, job types, or industries to ensure that you stay informed about relevant remote job opportunities.

Filter Job Listings: Use the filtering options available on remote work platforms to narrow down job listings based on your preferences, such as job type, location (remote), industry, and experience level. Filtering job listings can help you focus on remote job opportunities that align with your skills, experience, and career goals, saving you time and effort in your job search.

Research Companies: Before applying for remote job opportunities listed on remote work platforms, take the time to research the companies offering the positions. Visit their websites, read about their remote work policies and company culture, and explore employee reviews and testimonials to gain insights into their reputation as remote-friendly employers.

Customize Your Applications:
Tailor your job applications to each remote job opportunity to demonstrate your fit for the role and company. Highlight your relevant skills, experience, and accomplishments that align with the job requirements and responsibilities outlined in the job posting. Use keywords and phrases from the job description to optimize your application for applicant tracking systems (ATS) used by employers.

Network with Recruiters and Employers: Engage with recruiters, hiring managers, and employers on remote work platforms to expand your network and increase your visibility to remote-friendly companies. Connect with professionals who work for companies offering remote job opportunities, express your interest in remote work, and inquire about potential job openings or referrals.

Stay Active and Engaged: Stay active and engaged on remote work platforms by regularly updating your profile, applying for relevant job opportunities, and participating in discussions and forums related to remote work. Engage with other

remote professionals, share insights and experiences, and contribute value to the remote work community to build relationships and establish yourself as a credible remote job candidate.

Follow Up on Applications: After submitting your job applications through remote work platforms, follow up with the hiring managers or recruiters to express your continued interest in the position and inquire about the status of your application. Sending a polite and professional follow-up email or message demonstrates your proactive approach and enthusiasm for the role.

Overview of Popular Remote Work Platforms

In the ever-expanding landscape of remote work, several platforms have emerged as go-to destinations for individuals seeking legitimate work-from-home opportunities. These platforms serve as centralized hubs where remote job seekers can discover job listings, connect with remote-friendly companies, and access resources to support their remote work journey. Here's an overview of some of the most popular remote work platforms:

FlexJobs: FlexJobs is a leading online job board specializing in remote, freelance, and flexible job opportunities. With a curated database of remote job listings from reputable companies across various industries, FlexJobs offers a user-friendly platform for remote job seekers to find legitimate work-from-home opportunities. Job seekers can access job listings, company profiles, career resources, and personalized job search support through FlexJobs.

Remote.co: Remote.co is a platform that features remote job opportunities from companies of all sizes and industries. Their curated list of remote job listings includes full-time, part-time, and freelance positions, as well as remote-friendly companies that embrace distributed workforces. Remote.co provides resources, insights, and articles on remote work topics to support remote job seekers throughout their job search journey.

We Work Remotely: We Work Remotely is one of the largest remote job boards, featuring remote job opportunities in fields such as programming, design, marketing, and customer support. Their platform offers a wide range of remote job listings from reputable companies worldwide. Job seekers can explore job listings, subscribe to job alerts, and access resources on remote work best practices through We Work Remotely.

Virtual Vocations: Virtual Vocations is a job board specializing in telecommuting and remote job opportunities. Their platform features remote job listings across various industries, including healthcare, education, sales, and administration. Virtual Vocations offers job search tools, resume writing services, and career resources tailored to remote job seekers.

RemoteOK: RemoteOK is a remote job board that aggregates remote job listings from various sources, including company websites, job boards, and social media. Their platform features remote job opportunities in tech, marketing, design, and other fields, with options for full-time, part-time, and freelance remote work. RemoteOK allows users to filter job listings

by location, job type, and keyword to find remote jobs that match their preferences.

LinkedIn: LinkedIn is a professional networking platform that also serves as a valuable resource for finding remote job opportunities. Job seekers can search for remote job listings using LinkedIn's job search feature and filter results by location, job type, and industry. Additionally, LinkedIn allows users to follow companies that offer remote work options and join remote work-related groups and communities to connect with other remote professionals and stay updated on remote job openings.

Toptal: Toptal is a talent marketplace that connects companies with top freelancers in fields such as software development, design, finance, and project management. They offer remote job opportunities for freelancers to work on projects with clients from around the world. Freelancers can apply to join Toptal's network and access remote job opportunities through their platform.

These popular remote work platforms serve as valuable resources for individuals seeking legitimate work-from-home opportunities across various industries and job roles. By leveraging these platforms effectively, remote job seekers can access a diverse range of remote job opportunities, connect with remote-friendly companies, and navigate the remote work landscape with confidence.

Creating an Appealing Profile for Remote Work Platforms

Crafting an appealing profile on remote work platforms is essential for attracting the attention of employers and increasing your chances of landing legitimate work-from-home opportunities. Your profile serves as a digital representation of your skills, experience, and qualifications, so it's important to make it stand out and showcase your strengths effectively. Here are some tips for creating an appealing profile for remote work platforms:

Professional Profile Picture:
Choose a professional profile picture that presents you in a positive and approachable light. Avoid using overly casual or inappropriate photos, and opt for

a high-quality image that clearly shows your face. A professional headshot or a well-lit photo with a neutral background is ideal.

Compelling Headline: Craft a compelling headline that highlights your key skills, expertise, and the type of remote work opportunities you're seeking. Use keywords relevant to your desired job role and industry to optimize your profile for searchability. Your headline should grab the attention of employers and give them a clear idea of what you have to offer.

Detailed Work Experience: Provide detailed information about your work experience, including your job titles, responsibilities, and achievements. Highlight relevant remote work experience, if applicable, and emphasize any remote-friendly skills or accomplishments. Use bullet points or concise paragraphs to make your work experience easy to read and understand.

Skills and Expertise: List your skills and expertise prominently on your profile, focusing on those that are relevant to remote work and the job roles you're

69

targeting. Include both technical skills (e.g., software proficiency, programming languages) and soft skills (e.g., communication, time management) that are valuable in a remote work environment. Be honest about your skills and avoid exaggerating or misrepresenting your abilities.

Education and Certifications:

Provide information about your education, including your degree(s), certifications, and any relevant training or professional development courses you've completed. Highlight certifications or training related to remote work or specific job roles, such as remote project management certification or virtual collaboration training.

Personal Summary or Bio: Write a

concise and engaging personal summary or bio that introduces yourself to potential employers and highlights your career objectives, strengths, and motivations. Use this section to showcase your personality, values, and passion for remote work. Keep your summary focused and relevant to the job roles you're pursuing.

70

Portfolio or Work Samples: If applicable, include a portfolio of your work or samples of projects you've completed. This could include writing samples, design portfolios, code repositories, or links to websites or projects you've contributed to. Providing tangible examples of your work allows employers to assess your skills and expertise more effectively.

Testimonials and Recommendations: Request recommendations or testimonials from colleagues, clients, or supervisors who can attest to your skills, work ethic, and professionalism. Displaying positive endorsements on your profile adds credibility and reinforces your qualifications to potential employers.

Optimize for Keywords: Incorporate relevant keywords and phrases throughout your profile to improve its visibility in search results. Use terms related to your desired job role, industry, and remote work experience to increase the likelihood of your profile being discovered by employers searching for remote talent.

71

Regularly Update Your Profile:

Keep your profile up-to-date with the latest information about your skills, experience, and achievements. Regularly review and revise your profile to reflect any new skills or experiences you've gained, as well as any changes in your career objectives or job preferences.

Understanding Platform Etiquette and Rules

When navigating remote work platforms to find legitimate work-from-home opportunities, it's essential to understand and adhere to platform etiquette and rules to ensure a positive experience for both job seekers and employers. Each platform may have its own set of guidelines and community standards that govern user behavior and interactions. Here are some key aspects of platform etiquette and rules to keep in mind:

Read and Follow Guidelines:

Before using a remote work platform, take the time to read and familiarize yourself with the platform's guidelines, terms of service, and community rules. These guidelines outline acceptable behavior, prohibited activities, and the platform's expectations for users. Adhering to these guidelines is crucial for maintaining a positive and respectful environment for all users.

Be Professional and Courteous:

Maintain a professional and courteous demeanor when interacting with other users on the platform. Treat fellow job seekers, employers, and platform administrators with respect and professionalism in all communications. Avoid using offensive language, engaging in heated debates, or making derogatory remarks that could reflect negatively on your reputation.

Provide Accurate Information:

Ensure that the information you provide on your profile and in job applications is accurate, truthful, and up-to-date. Misrepresenting your skills, experience, or qualifications can damage your credibility and reputation on the platform. Be transparent about your capabilities and background to build trust with potential employers.

Respect Privacy and Confidentiality:
Respect the privacy and confidentiality of other users' information and communications on the platform. Avoid sharing sensitive or confidential information without permission and refrain from disclosing personal details or contact information in public forums or discussions. Protecting privacy and confidentiality is essential for maintaining trust and security within the platform community.

Engage Constructively:
Participate in discussions, forums, and community activities on the platform in a constructive and positive manner. Offer helpful insights, share relevant resources, and contribute value to discussions related to remote work topics. Avoid spamming, trolling, or engaging in disruptive behavior that detracts from the platform's purpose and goals.

Follow Application Guidelines:
When applying for remote job opportunities on the platform, carefully review and follow the application guidelines provided by the employer. Submit your application

materials in the format and manner specified by the employer, and ensure that you provide all requested information and documents accurately and completely. Failure to follow application guidelines could result in your application being overlooked or disqualified.

Report Violations Appropriately:

If you encounter any violations of platform guidelines or community rules, report them to the platform administrators or moderators promptly and appropriately. Most platforms have mechanisms in place for reporting inappropriate behavior, spam, scams, or other violations. Reporting violations helps maintain the integrity and safety of the platform community for all users.

Be Patient and Persistent: Finding

legitimate remote work opportunities may take time and persistence, so remain patient and persistent in your job search efforts. Keep refining your profile, networking with other users, and applying for relevant job opportunities on the platform. By staying proactive and engaged, you can increase your chances of finding legitimate work-from-home

**opportunities that align with your skills and
preferences.**

CHAPTER 4

DEVELOPING REMOTE WORK SKILLS

Remote work requires a unique set of skills and competencies to succeed in a virtual environment. Whether you're transitioning to remote work for the first time or looking to enhance your existing remote work skills, developing key competencies is essential for thriving in a remote work setting. Here are some essential remote work skills to develop:

Communication Skills: Effective communication is critical in remote work settings where face-to-face interactions are limited. Develop strong written and verbal communication skills to convey your ideas clearly and concisely. Practice active listening, ask clarifying questions, and use collaboration tools effectively to communicate with colleagues and managers.

Time Management: Remote work requires strong time management skills to stay organized, prioritize tasks, and meet deadlines without direct supervision. Develop strategies for managing your time effectively, such as creating schedules, setting goals, and using time-tracking tools to monitor your progress. Prioritize tasks based on importance and urgency, and avoid procrastination to maximize productivity.

Self-Discipline and Motivation:

Working remotely requires self-discipline and motivation to stay focused and productive without the structure and accountability of a traditional office environment. Develop self-discipline by establishing a dedicated workspace, setting boundaries, and adhering to a regular work routine. Find ways to stay motivated, such as setting goals, rewarding yourself for accomplishments, and maintaining a healthy work-life balance.

Adaptability and Flexibility:

Remote work environments are often dynamic and unpredictable, requiring adaptability and flexibility to navigate changes and challenges effectively. Develop resilience and flexibility to adapt to new technologies, workflows, and work processes. Embrace change as an opportunity for growth and learning, and remain open to new ideas and ways of working.

Tech Savviness: Remote work relies heavily on technology for communication, collaboration, and productivity. Develop proficiency in using remote work tools and platforms, such as video conferencing software, project management tools, document sharing platforms, and instant messaging apps. Stay up-to-date with technological advancements and seek opportunities to enhance your tech skills through training and self-directed learning.

Problem-Solving Skills: Remote work environments may present unique challenges and obstacles that require problem-solving skills to overcome. Develop critical thinking and problem-solving skills to identify issues, analyze root causes, and develop solutions independently or collaboratively with colleagues. Approach challenges with a proactive and solutions-oriented mindset to drive progress and innovation.

Collaboration and Teamwork: Effective collaboration and teamwork are

essential for remote teams to achieve their goals and deliver results. Develop skills for building relationships, fostering trust, and collaborating with colleagues across geographical distances. Practice inclusive communication, share knowledge and resources, and contribute to a positive team culture that values collaboration and mutual support.

Remote Work Tools and Technologies:

Familiarize yourself with remote work tools and technologies commonly used in virtual work environments. Learn how to use video conferencing platforms, project management tools, collaborative document editing software, and other remote work tools efficiently. Stay updated on new tools and technologies that can enhance productivity and communication in remote teams.

Time Management and Productivity Techniques for Remote Work

Remote work offers flexibility and autonomy, but it also requires discipline and effective time management to stay productive and maintain work-life balance. Here are some time management and productivity techniques tailored for remote workers:

Establish a Routine: Set a consistent daily schedule for your remote work hours, including start and end times, breaks, and dedicated time for tasks. Establishing a routine helps create structure and discipline, making it easier to transition into work mode and stay focused throughout the day.

Create a Dedicated Workspace: Designate a specific area in your home as your remote work environment. Ideally, this space should be quiet, comfortable, and free from distractions. Having a dedicated workspace signals to your brain that it's time to focus and helps minimize interruptions during work hours.

Set Clear Goals and Priorities: Define your daily, weekly, and long-term goals to guide your work and prioritize tasks effectively. Break down larger projects into smaller, manageable tasks and set realistic deadlines for completing

81

them. Focus on high-priority tasks that align with your objectives and contribute to your overall productivity.

Use Time-Blocking Techniques:
Allocate specific blocks of time on your calendar for different tasks, projects, and activities. Time-blocking helps structure your day, prevents multitasking, and ensures that you allocate sufficient time to important tasks. Stick to your time blocks as much as possible to maintain focus and productivity.

Limit Distractions: Minimize
distractions in your remote work environment to maximize your productivity. Turn off notifications on your phone and computer, close unnecessary browser tabs, and use productivity apps or browser extensions to block distracting websites or social media during work hours. Create boundaries with family members or roommates to minimize interruptions while you work.

Practice the Pomodoro Technique: The Pomodoro Technique involves working in focused intervals (typically 25 minutes) followed by short

breaks (5 minutes). Set a timer for each work interval, and focus solely on the task at hand until the timer goes off. Take a short break to rest and recharge before starting the next interval. Repeat this cycle throughout your workday to maintain productivity and prevent burnout.

Prioritize Self-Care: Take regular breaks throughout the day to rest, recharge, and avoid burnout. Use your breaks to stretch, go for a walk, meditate, or engage in activities that help you relax and recharge. Prioritize self-care practices such as exercise, healthy eating, and adequate sleep to maintain your physical and mental well-being, which are essential for sustained productivity.

Communicate Effectively with Your Team: Clear and open communication is crucial for remote teams to collaborate effectively and stay aligned on goals and priorities. Use collaboration tools such as video conferencing, instant messaging, and project management platforms to communicate with colleagues, share updates, and coordinate tasks. Schedule regular check-ins and team

meetings to stay connected and foster a sense of camaraderie among remote team members.

Reflect and Adjust: Regularly reflect on your time management and productivity habits to identify what's working well and where you can improve. Experiment with different techniques and strategies to find what works best for you in your remote work environment. Be flexible and willing to adjust your approach as needed to optimize your productivity and well-being.

Seek Support and Accountability: Surround yourself with a supportive network of colleagues, mentors, or accountability partners who can provide encouragement, advice, and accountability in your remote work journey. Share your goals and challenges with trusted individuals who can offer guidance and support to help you stay on track and overcome obstacles.

Communication Skills for Remote Teams

Effective communication is essential for remote teams to collaborate, coordinate tasks, and maintain cohesion in a virtual work environment. Remote work relies heavily on written and verbal communication, as well as digital tools and technologies to facilitate interactions among team members. Here are some key communication skills for remote teams to cultivate:

Clear and Concise Communication:
Remote communication requires clarity and conciseness to ensure messages are understood effectively. Use clear and straightforward language when communicating with team members, avoiding ambiguity and jargon that may lead to misunderstandings. Be concise in your messages, getting to the point quickly while providing all necessary information.

Active Listening:
Active listening is crucial in remote team communication to demonstrate empathy, understanding, and engagement with colleagues. Practice active listening by focusing on what the speaker is saying, asking clarifying questions, and providing feedback to ensure mutual understanding. Avoid

interrupting and multitasking during virtual meetings to show respect and attention to the speaker.

Written Communication Skills:
Written communication skills are paramount in remote work environments, where much of the communication occurs through emails, instant messages, and project management platforms. Develop strong written communication skills, including grammar, spelling, and punctuation, to convey your ideas clearly and professionally. Use proper formatting, bullet points, and headings to structure your written messages for clarity and readability.

Virtual Meeting Etiquette:
Virtual meetings play a significant role in remote team communication, requiring adherence to virtual meeting etiquette to ensure efficiency and professionalism. Set expectations for virtual meetings regarding punctuality, agenda setting, and participation guidelines. Use video conferencing tools effectively, including muting microphones when not speaking, avoiding distractions, and maintaining eye

contact to simulate face-to-face interactions.

Empathy and Emotional Intelligence:
Cultivate empathy and emotional intelligence in remote team communication to understand and respond to colleagues' emotions and perspectives effectively. Acknowledge and validate others' feelings, show empathy towards their challenges and concerns, and be supportive and understanding in your interactions. Embrace diversity and inclusivity in communication, respecting cultural differences and individual preferences.

Collaborative Communication:
Foster a collaborative communication culture within your remote team, emphasizing openness, transparency, and teamwork. Encourage active participation and contribution from all team members, regardless of their roles or seniority. Use collaborative tools and platforms to facilitate communication, brainstorming, and idea sharing in virtual team environments.

Feedback and Recognition:

Provide constructive feedback and recognition to your remote team members to promote growth, development, and motivation. Offer feedback on performance, projects, and contributions in a constructive and respectful manner, focusing on specific behaviors and outcomes. Recognize and celebrate achievements, milestones, and successes openly to boost morale and reinforce positive behaviors.

Conflict Resolution Skills: Conflict

may arise in remote teams due to miscommunications, differing opinions, or misunderstandings. Develop conflict resolution skills to address conflicts proactively and constructively. Encourage open dialogue, active listening, and empathy in resolving conflicts, focusing on finding mutually beneficial solutions and maintaining positive relationships within the team.

Adaptability to Communication

Tools: Remote teams rely on a variety of communication tools and technologies to collaborate effectively, including email, instant messaging, video conferencing, and project management platforms. Be adaptable and proficient in using these communication tools, staying updated on their features and functionalities to leverage them optimally in remote team interactions.

Continuous Improvement:

Communication skills require continuous improvement and refinement to meet the evolving needs of remote teams. Seek feedback from colleagues, reflect on your communication experiences, and actively pursue opportunities for learning and development. Stay informed about best practices, trends, and emerging technologies in remote team communication to enhance your skills and effectiveness as a remote team member.

Self-Motivation and Accountability Strategies for Remote Work

Remote work offers flexibility and autonomy, but it also requires self-motivation and accountability to stay focused, productive, and on track with goals and deadlines. Working from home presents unique challenges, such as distractions and isolation, that can impact motivation and accountability. Here are some strategies to cultivate self-motivation and accountability in remote work:

Set Clear Goals: Establish clear, achievable goals for your work to provide direction and purpose. Break down larger goals into smaller, actionable tasks with deadlines to create a roadmap for your work. Set both short-term and long-term goals to maintain motivation and track progress over time.

Create a Routine: Establish a daily routine that mimics the structure and schedule of a traditional office environment. Set regular work hours and designate specific times for starting and ending work, taking breaks, and engaging in non-work activities. Stick to your routine as much as possible to create consistency and stability in your remote workday.

Designate a Dedicated Workspace: Create a dedicated workspace in your home that is free from distractions and conducive to productivity.

Choose a quiet, comfortable area with adequate lighting and ergonomic furniture where you can focus on your work without interruptions. Keep your workspace organized and clutter-free to minimize distractions and promote concentration.

Stay Organized: Maintain organization in your work by using tools and systems to manage tasks, deadlines, and priorities. Use to-do lists, task managers, or project management tools to track your tasks and deadlines effectively. Break down tasks into smaller, manageable steps, and prioritize them based on importance and urgency to stay focused and productive.

Eliminate Distractions: Identify and eliminate distractions in your work environment to maintain focus and productivity. Minimize interruptions by turning off notifications, closing unnecessary tabs or apps, and setting boundaries with family members or roommates. Use productivity tools or browser extensions to block distracting websites during focused work sessions.

Establish Accountability Systems: Hold yourself accountable for

91

your work by establishing accountability systems and accountability partners. Set deadlines for tasks and projects, and hold yourself accountable for meeting them. Share your goals and progress with a trusted colleague, mentor, or friend who can provide support, encouragement, and accountability.

Practice Self-discipline: Cultivate self-discipline to resist procrastination and stay focused on your work. Develop habits and rituals that support productivity, such as starting your day with a morning routine, taking regular breaks, and avoiding multitasking. Stay committed to your goals and priorities, even when faced with distractions or challenges.

Celebrate Progress and Achievements: Acknowledge and celebrate your progress and achievements to stay motivated and inspired. Recognize milestones, accomplishments, and successes, no matter how small, and celebrate them as a reflection of your hard work and dedication. Reward yourself for reaching goals or completing tasks with

breaks, treats, or other incentives to reinforce positive behaviors.

Seek Inspiration and Support:

Surround yourself with inspiration and support to fuel your motivation and resilience. Connect with like-minded individuals in remote work communities, online forums, or social media groups to share experiences, insights, and encouragement. Seek inspiration from books, podcasts, or articles on productivity, motivation, and personal development to stay inspired and motivated.

Reflect and Adjust: Regularly reflect

on your self-motivation and accountability strategies to identify what is working well and what can be improved. Assess your progress towards your goals, evaluate your productivity habits, and adjust your approach as needed to optimize your performance and effectiveness in remote work.

CHAPTER 5

MAINTAINING WORK-LIFE BALANCE IN REMOTE WORK

Remote work offers flexibility and autonomy, but it also blurs the boundaries between work and personal life, making it challenging to maintain a healthy work-life balance. Without the physical separation of a traditional office, remote workers may find themselves working longer hours, experiencing burnout, or struggling to disconnect from work. Here are some strategies to maintain work-life balance while working remotely:

Set Boundaries: Establish clear boundaries between work and personal life to create separation and structure in your remote workday. Define specific work hours and non-work hours, and communicate them to your colleagues, clients, and family members. Resist the temptation to work outside of your designated work hours and respect your personal time.

Create a Dedicated Workspace:
Designate a dedicated workspace in your home that is separate from your living areas. Set up a comfortable and ergonomic workspace with minimal distractions where you can focus on your work during work hours. When you're done working, leave your workspace to signal the end of the workday and transition into personal time.

Stick to a Schedule: Maintain a consistent daily schedule that includes set start and end times for work, as well as designated break times and downtime. Structure your day with a balance of work-related tasks, personal activities, and leisure time to create rhythm and routine in your remote workday. Stick to your schedule as much as possible to create predictability and stability in your routine.

Take Regular Breaks: Prioritize taking regular breaks throughout your workday to rest, recharge, and prevent burnout. Schedule short breaks between tasks to stretch, move around, and refresh your mind. Use longer breaks for meals, exercise, or relaxation to rejuvenate and replenish your energy levels. Incorporating

breaks into your routine helps maintain focus, productivity, and well-being throughout the day.

Set Realistic Expectations:

Manage your workload and set realistic expectations for what you can accomplish in a given day or week. Avoid overcommitting yourself to tasks or projects that exceed your capacity or availability. Communicate openly with your colleagues or clients about your workload, deadlines, and priorities to manage expectations effectively.

Practice Time Management:

Develop effective time management skills to prioritize tasks, allocate time efficiently, and maximize productivity. Use time-blocking techniques to schedule focused work sessions and designate specific time slots for different activities. Set time limits for tasks to prevent them from expanding indefinitely and encroaching on your personal time.

Unplug and Disconnect: Create

boundaries around technology use and disconnect from work-related devices and communication channels outside of work hours. Turn off notifications, mute work-related apps, and set boundaries with colleagues or clients about when you are available for work-related communication. Use "do not disturb" modes or automated responses to signal your availability status during non-work hours.

Engage in Self-care: Prioritize self-care practices to nurture your physical, mental, and emotional well-being. Make time for activities that promote relaxation, stress relief, and fulfillment, such as exercise, hobbies, meditation, or spending time outdoors. Invest in self-care routines that replenish your energy and resilience, allowing you to show up as your best self in both work and personal life.

Set Personal Goals: Establish personal goals and priorities outside of work to maintain a sense of balance and fulfillment in your life. Set goals related to health, relationships, hobbies, or personal development and allocate time and resources to pursue them. Incorporate activities that align with your personal values and interests into your daily or weekly routine to cultivate a sense of purpose and fulfillment beyond work.

97

Seek Support and Connection: Connect with others who understand the challenges of remote work and seek support from friends, family, or peers in similar situations. Share experiences, insights, and strategies for maintaining work-life balance in remote work environments. Join online communities, forums, or virtual meetups for remote workers to exchange ideas, resources, and support.

Setting Boundaries Between Work and Personal Life in Remote Work

Remote work offers flexibility and autonomy, but it also blurs the lines between work and personal life, making it essential to establish clear boundaries to maintain a healthy balance. Without the physical separation of a traditional office, remote workers may find themselves constantly connected to work, leading to burnout and decreased well-being. Here are some strategies for setting boundaries between work and personal life in remote work:

Designate a Workspace: Create a dedicated workspace in your home where you can focus on work without distractions. Choose a quiet, comfortable area away from common living spaces and establish it as your designated workspace. When you're in your workspace, treat it as if you're in a traditional office, and when you're done working, leave the space to signal the end of the workday.

Set Clear Work Hours: Define specific work hours and communicate them to your colleagues, clients, and family members. Establish a consistent schedule that aligns with your peak productivity times and personal commitments. Stick to your work hours as much as possible, and avoid the temptation to work outside of these designated times.

Communicate Boundaries: Clearly communicate your boundaries around work availability, communication preferences, and response times to your colleagues and clients. Set expectations about when you are available for work-related communication and when you are not. Use automated responses, calendar blocking,

or status updates to signal your availability status to others.

Establish Transition Routines:

Create transition routines to bookend your workday and signal the transition between work and personal life. Start your day with a morning routine that prepares you for work, such as exercise, meditation, or planning your day. Similarly, end your workday with a routine that helps you unwind and transition into personal time, such as going for a walk, practicing relaxation techniques, or spending time with loved ones.

Limit Work-related Communication:

Set boundaries around work-related communication outside of work hours to prevent work from encroaching on personal time. Turn off notifications, mute work-related apps, and establish "do not disturb" times when you are unavailable for work-related communication. Communicate your boundaries to colleagues and clients, and respectfully decline non-urgent requests that can wait until the next workday.

100

Schedule Breaks and Downtime:

Prioritize breaks and downtime throughout your workday to rest, recharge, and prevent burnout. Schedule regular breaks between tasks to stretch, move around, and refresh your mind. Use longer breaks for meals, exercise, or leisure activities to rejuvenate and replenish your energy levels. Incorporating breaks into your routine helps maintain focus, productivity, and well-being throughout the day.

Create Personal Time Blocks:

Block off dedicated personal time in your schedule for activities that nourish your well-being and fulfillment outside of work. Allocate time for hobbies, exercise, socializing, or relaxation, and treat these activities as non-negotiable commitments. Schedule personal time blocks as you would work meetings or appointments, and prioritize them as essential elements of your daily or weekly routine.

Practice Saying No: Learn to say no

to work-related requests or commitments that conflict with your personal boundaries or priorities. Prioritize your well-being and balance by setting limits on your workload, availability, and obligations. Communicate your boundaries respectfully but assertively, and offer alternative solutions or compromises when necessary.

Seek Support and Accountability: Enlist the support of friends, family, or peers to help you maintain boundaries and accountability in your remote work. Share your goals, challenges, and strategies for work-life balance with trusted individuals who can provide encouragement, accountability, and perspective. Lean on your support network for guidance, feedback, and validation as you navigate the challenges of remote work.

Regularly Evaluate and Adjust: Regularly evaluate your boundaries and work-life balance to assess what is working well and what can be improved. Reflect on your experiences, needs, and priorities, and adjust your boundaries as needed to maintain a healthy balance. Be flexible and adaptive in refining your boundaries based on changes in your workload, personal circumstances, or well-being.

Creating a Productive Workspace at Home

Designing an effective and conducive workspace is crucial for remote workers to maximize productivity, focus, and comfort while working from home. A well-designed workspace can help minimize distractions, promote concentration, and create a conducive environment for remote work success. Here are some tips for creating a productive workspace at home:

Choose the Right Location: Select a quiet and dedicated area in your home that is conducive to focused work. Ideally, choose a separate room or corner away from high-traffic areas, household noise, and distractions. Consider factors such as natural light, ventilation, and privacy when choosing your workspace location.

Invest in Ergonomic Furniture: Invest in ergonomic furniture, such as a comfortable desk and chair, to support good posture and reduce the risk of discomfort or injury during long hours of work. Choose a desk and chair that are adjustable to your height and preferences, and consider adding ergonomic

103

accessories such as a keyboard tray, monitor stand, or footrest for added comfort.

Set Up Proper Lighting: Ensure adequate lighting in your workspace to reduce eye strain and promote alertness and productivity. Position your desk near a window to take advantage of natural light, or use task lighting such as a desk lamp or overhead light to illuminate your workspace effectively. Adjust the lighting to minimize glare and shadows on your computer screen.

Organize and Declutter: Keep your workspace organized and clutter-free to create a clean and functional environment for work. Use storage solutions such as shelves, cabinets, or storage bins to keep your desk and surrounding area tidy and organized. Minimize distractions by clearing away unnecessary items and keeping only essential tools and supplies within reach.

Personalize Your Space: Personalize your workspace with elements that inspire and motivate you to work productively. Add personal touches such as

photos, artwork, plants, or inspirational quotes to make your workspace feel inviting and personalized. Choose decor that reflects your personality and preferences while maintaining a professional and organized appearance.

Optimize Technology Setup: Set up your technology and equipment in a way that supports productivity and efficiency in your remote work tasks. Position your computer monitor at eye level to reduce neck strain, and ensure that your keyboard and mouse are positioned comfortably within reach. Arrange cables and cords neatly to minimize clutter and prevent tripping hazards.

Create a Distraction-Free Zone: Minimize distractions in your workspace to maintain focus and concentration during work hours. Set boundaries with family members or roommates about respecting your workspace and minimizing interruptions during work time. Use noise-cancelling headphones or background music to mask distracting noises and create a focused environment.

Establish Work-Life Boundaries:

Separate your work area from your living space to create clear boundaries between work and personal life. Designate specific times for work and non-work activities, and avoid using your workspace for non-work-related tasks or activities. When you're done working, physically leave your workspace to signal the end of the workday and transition into personal time.

Create a Productive Atmosphere:

Foster a productive atmosphere in your workspace by incorporating elements that enhance focus and creativity. Play instrumental music or white noise to create a calming ambiance, or diffuse essential oils with invigorating scents such as peppermint or citrus to boost alertness and concentration. Experiment with different sensory cues to find what works best for you.

Regularly Maintain and Refresh Your Workspace:

Regularly maintain and refresh your workspace to keep it clean, organized, and conducive to productivity. Take time to declutter, dust, and rearrange your workspace as needed to maintain a fresh and inspiring environment for work. Incorporate regular breaks to stretch, move around, and refresh your mind and body throughout the day.

Managing Stress and Burnout in Remote Work

Remote work offers flexibility and autonomy, but it also comes with its unique challenges, including increased stress and the risk of burnout. Without the physical separation of a traditional office environment, remote workers may find it challenging to disconnect from work, set boundaries, and manage work-related stress effectively. Here are some strategies for managing stress and preventing burnout in remote work:

Set Realistic Expectations:

Manage your workload and set realistic expectations for what you can accomplish within a given timeframe. Avoid overcommitting yourself to tasks or projects that exceed your capacity or availability. Communicate openly with your colleagues or clients about your workload, deadlines, and priorities to manage expectations effectively.

Establish Work-Life Boundaries:
Create clear boundaries between work and personal life to prevent work from encroaching on your personal time. Designate specific times for work and non-work activities, and avoid working outside of your designated work hours. When you're done working, physically leave your workspace to signal the end of the workday and transition into personal time.

Take Regular Breaks: Prioritize
taking regular breaks throughout your workday to rest, recharge, and prevent burnout. Schedule short breaks between tasks to stretch, move around, and refresh your mind. Use longer breaks for meals, exercise, or relaxation to rejuvenate and replenish your energy levels. Incorporating breaks into your routine helps maintain focus, productivity, and well-being throughout the day.

Practice Self-care: Prioritize self-
care practices to nurture your physical, mental, and emotional well-being. Make time for activities that promote relaxation,

stress relief, and fulfillment, such as exercise, meditation, hobbies, or spending time outdoors. Invest in self-care routines that replenish your energy and resilience, allowing you to show up as your best self in both work and personal life.

Stay Connected: Maintain connection and support with colleagues, friends, and family members to combat feelings of isolation and loneliness in remote work. Schedule virtual coffee breaks, team meetings, or social activities to stay connected with your colleagues and foster a sense of camaraderie. Reach out to friends and family for social support, encouragement, and companionship outside of work.

Seek Professional Support: If you're struggling with stress or burnout, don't hesitate to seek professional support from a therapist, counselor, or mental health professional. Reach out to your employer's Employee Assistance Program (EAP) or explore teletherapy options for remote support. Talking to a mental health professional can provide valuable strategies and resources for managing stress and improving well-being.

Practice Mindfulness and Relaxation Techniques: Incorporate mindfulness and relaxation techniques into your daily routine to reduce stress and promote a sense of calm and balance. Practice deep breathing exercises, meditation, or progressive muscle relaxation to release tension and stress from your body and mind. Set aside time for mindfulness practices to cultivate present moment awareness and reduce anxiety and overwhelm.

Limit Screen Time and Digital Overload: Minimize exposure to screens and digital devices outside of work hours to prevent digital overload and mental fatigue. Set boundaries around technology use, such as turning off work-related notifications or setting designated screen-free times. Engage in offline activities that promote relaxation and enjoyment, such as reading, crafting, or spending time with loved ones.

Reflect and Reassess Regularly: Regularly reflect on your stress levels, well-being, and work-life balance to identify areas for improvement and adjustment.

110

Assess your workload, priorities, and self-care practices, and make necessary changes to optimize your stress management strategies. Prioritize activities and commitments that align with your values and well-being, and let go of unnecessary stressors or obligations.

Seek Balance and Flexibility:

Embrace a mindset of balance and flexibility in your approach to remote work, recognizing that achieving perfect balance is an ongoing process. Be gentle with yourself and practice self-compassion when facing challenges or setbacks. Allow yourself to adapt and adjust as needed to find a balance that works for you and supports your overall well-being and success in remote work.

CHAPTER 6

OVERCOMING REMOTE WORK CHALLENGES

While remote work offers numerous benefits, it also presents unique challenges that remote workers must navigate to succeed in a virtual work environment. From communication barriers to feelings of isolation, overcoming these challenges requires proactive strategies and a resilient mindset. Here are some common remote work challenges and strategies for overcoming them:

Communication Barriers: Remote work can sometimes lead to communication barriers due to the lack of face-to-face interaction. To overcome this challenge, remote workers should prioritize clear and frequent communication using various channels such as video calls, instant messaging, and email. Establishing regular check-ins with team members and utilizing collaboration tools can also enhance communication and collaboration in remote teams.

Feelings of Isolation: Working remotely can sometimes lead to feelings of isolation and loneliness, especially for those who thrive on social interaction. To combat isolation, remote workers should proactively seek opportunities for social connection and interaction. This can include participating in virtual team meetings, joining online communities or forums for remote workers, and scheduling virtual coffee breaks or social activities with colleagues.

Lack of Boundaries: One common challenge in remote work is the blurring of boundaries between work and personal life. To address this challenge, remote workers should establish clear boundaries between work and non-work activities. This can involve setting specific work hours, creating a dedicated workspace, and developing rituals or routines to signal the start and end of the workday.

Distractions at Home: Working from home can sometimes be accompanied by distractions such as household chores, family members, or pets. To minimize distractions, remote workers should create a conducive work environment by setting up a designated workspace that is free from distractions. Using productivity techniques such as time blocking and implementing strategies to manage interruptions can also help remote workers stay focused and productive.

Tech Issues and Connectivity Problems:
Technical issues and connectivity problems can disrupt remote work and impact productivity. To address this challenge, remote workers should ensure they have reliable internet connectivity and access to necessary technology tools and resources. Having backup plans in place, such as alternative internet connections or contingency communication channels, can also help mitigate the impact of tech issues.

Work-Life Imbalance:
Achieving work-life balance can be challenging in remote work, as the boundaries between work and personal life can become blurred. To overcome this challenge, remote workers should prioritize self-care and set boundaries around their work schedule. This may involve scheduling regular

breaks, establishing a routine, and making time for activities outside of work that promote relaxation and well-being.

Collaboration and Teamwork:

Collaborating effectively with remote team members can sometimes be challenging due to differences in time zones, cultural backgrounds, or communication styles. To address this challenge, remote workers should focus on building trust, fostering open communication, and embracing diversity within their remote teams. Utilizing collaboration tools and establishing clear expectations for teamwork and accountability can also enhance collaboration in remote teams.

Professional Development and Networking:

Remote workers may sometimes face challenges in accessing professional development opportunities and networking events that are typically available in traditional office settings. To overcome this challenge, remote workers should actively seek out remote-friendly professional development resources, such as online courses, webinars, and virtual conferences. Engaging with remote work communities and networking groups can also provide valuable opportunities for connecting with peers and expanding professional networks.

Dealing with Isolation and Loneliness in Remote Work

Remote work offers flexibility and autonomy, but it can also lead to feelings of isolation and loneliness for some individuals. Without the social interactions and camaraderie found in traditional office settings, remote workers may struggle to connect with others and experience a sense of belonging. To combat isolation and loneliness in remote work, consider implementing the following strategies:

Build a Support Network: Actively seek out opportunities to connect with other remote workers and build a support network. Join online communities, forums, or social media groups for remote workers to share experiences, exchange ideas, and provide support to one another. Participate in virtual meetups, networking events, or coworking sessions to connect with like-minded individuals and foster relationships.

Schedule Regular Check-Ins:

Maintain regular communication with colleagues, friends, and family members to combat feelings of isolation. Schedule virtual coffee breaks, team meetings, or social activities to stay connected with coworkers and maintain a sense of camaraderie. Reach out to friends and family for regular check-ins, phone calls, or video chats to nurture relationships and stay connected.

Participate in Virtual Events:

Take advantage of virtual events, workshops, and conferences to connect with others and engage in professional or personal development opportunities. Attend webinars, online courses, or virtual networking events related to your industry or interests to expand your knowledge, skills, and network. Engaging in virtual events can provide opportunities for connection and collaboration with others in remote work environments.

Seek Social Interaction:

Incorporate social interaction into your daily routine to combat feelings of loneliness and isolation. Schedule virtual lunches, coffee dates, or happy hours with friends, family, or colleagues to maintain social connections and foster a sense of community. Consider joining local clubs, classes, or hobby groups to meet new people and engage in shared interests outside of work.

Explore Coworking Spaces:
Consider working from coworking spaces or shared office environments occasionally to break up the monotony of working from home and connect with other professionals. Coworking spaces offer opportunities for networking, collaboration, and social interaction with other remote workers and entrepreneurs. Reserve a desk or workspace at a coworking space for a change of scenery and a sense of community.

Engage in Volunteer Work: Get
involved in volunteer work or community service activities to connect with others and make a positive impact in your community. Volunteer opportunities can provide opportunities for social interaction, networking, and meaningful connections with others who share your values and interests. Explore virtual volunteering

118

opportunities or local community organizations to find opportunities to give back and connect with others.

Practice Self-care: Prioritize self-care practices to nurture your well-being and resilience in the face of isolation and loneliness. Make time for activities that promote relaxation, stress relief, and fulfillment, such as exercise, meditation, hobbies, or spending time outdoors. Invest in self-care routines that replenish your energy and support your mental and emotional health, allowing you to navigate the challenges of isolation with resilience and positivity.

Seek Professional Support: If feelings of isolation and loneliness persist, don't hesitate to seek professional support from a therapist, counselor, or mental health professional. Talking to a professional can provide valuable strategies and resources for managing loneliness and improving well-being. Reach out to your employer's Employee Assistance Program (EAP) or explore teletherapy options for remote support.

119

Addressing Technological Issues and Connectivity Problems

Remote work relies heavily on technology and connectivity, making it essential for remote workers to address technological issues and connectivity problems effectively. Technical glitches and connectivity issues can disrupt workflow, hinder productivity, and create frustration for remote workers. To address these challenges and maintain smooth operations in remote work, consider implementing the following strategies:

Perform Regular System Checks: Conduct regular checks of your hardware, software, and internet connection to identify and address potential issues proactively. Check for updates to your operating system, software applications, and antivirus programs to ensure they are up-to-date and functioning properly. Test your internet speed and connectivity regularly to detect any fluctuations or disruptions.

Invest in Reliable Technology:

Invest in reliable technology tools and equipment to support your remote work needs. Ensure you have a reliable computer or laptop with adequate processing power, memory, and storage capacity for your work tasks. Use high-quality peripherals such as a keyboard, mouse, and webcam to enhance your productivity and comfort. Consider investing in a reliable internet service provider (ISP) and upgrading your internet plan if necessary to ensure stable and high-speed connectivity.

Backup Data Regularly: Protect

your work data and documents by implementing a regular backup routine. Use cloud-based storage solutions or external hard drives to backup your files regularly and prevent data loss in the event of hardware failure or system crashes. Set up automatic backup schedules or reminders to ensure your data is backed up consistently and securely.

Utilize Tech Support Resources:

Familiarize yourself with the tech support resources available to you, such as IT support from your employer, online

121

troubleshooting guides, or manufacturer's customer support services. Reach out to your employer's IT department or helpdesk for assistance with technical issues related to work-related software, systems, or equipment. Use online forums, communities, or knowledge bases to find solutions to common technical problems or seek advice from other users.

Implement Redundancy Measures:
Implement redundancy measures to mitigate the impact of technology failures or connectivity issues. For example, use backup internet connections such as mobile hotspots or secondary ISPs to maintain connectivity in case of network outages. Keep backup devices or equipment on hand in case of hardware failure, such as a spare laptop or mobile device.

Troubleshoot Connectivity Problems:
Troubleshoot connectivity problems systematically to identify and resolve issues effectively. Start by checking your internet connection, router, and modem to ensure they are working correctly. Test connectivity on different

devices or networks to isolate the source of the problem. Troubleshoot common connectivity issues such as Wi-Fi interference, signal strength, or network congestion to restore stable internet connectivity.

Use Communication Alternatives: In the event of internet or connectivity issues, utilize alternative communication methods to stay connected with colleagues and clients. Use mobile data or phone calls for essential communication if your internet connection is down. Keep a list of backup communication channels such as email, messaging apps, or alternative video conferencing platforms to use in case of emergencies.

Stay Informed About Tech Trends: Stay informed about emerging technologies, trends, and best practices in remote work to stay ahead of potential technological challenges. Keep up-to-date with industry news, software updates, and cybersecurity threats to anticipate and address potential issues proactively. Engage in professional development

opportunities such as online courses, webinars, or workshops to enhance your technical skills and knowledge.

Managing Conflicts and Misunderstandings in Remote Teams

Working in remote teams presents unique challenges in communication and collaboration, which can sometimes lead to conflicts and misunderstandings among team members. Addressing conflicts and resolving misunderstandings effectively is essential for maintaining harmony and productivity in remote work environments. Here are some strategies for managing conflicts and misunderstandings in remote teams:

Establish Clear Communication Guidelines:
Set clear communication guidelines and expectations for remote team members to follow. Establish preferred communication channels, response times, and etiquette for email, instant messaging, and video calls. Clarify how team members should communicate about project updates, deadlines, and

feedback to minimize misunderstandings and promote effective communication.

Encourage Open Communication:

Foster a culture of open communication and transparency within the remote team, where team members feel comfortable expressing their thoughts, concerns, and ideas. Encourage team members to voice their opinions, ask questions, and provide feedback openly and constructively. Create opportunities for regular check-ins, team meetings, or virtual brainstorming sessions to facilitate communication and collaboration.

Practice Active Listening:

Encourage active listening among team members to ensure mutual understanding and empathy in communication. Encourage team members to listen attentively to one another, ask clarifying questions, and paraphrase to confirm understanding. Avoid making assumptions or jumping to conclusions, and seek to understand the perspectives and motivations of others before responding.

Clarify Expectations and Roles:

Clarify expectations and roles within the

125

remote team to minimize confusion and ambiguity. Clearly define each team member's responsibilities, tasks, and goals, and communicate them effectively to ensure alignment and accountability. Establish clear workflows, deadlines, and deliverables for projects to prevent misunderstandings and conflicts over responsibilities.

Address Issues Promptly: Address conflicts and misunderstandings promptly and proactively to prevent escalation and maintain positive working relationships. Encourage team members to address issues directly and respectfully with the individuals involved, rather than letting grievances fester or escalate. Provide support and guidance to team members in resolving conflicts constructively and finding mutually acceptable solutions.

Use Conflict Resolution Strategies: Utilize conflict resolution strategies to address conflicts and misunderstandings effectively within the remote team. Encourage open dialogue and negotiation to find common ground and resolve differences collaboratively.

Consider using techniques such as active listening, perspective-taking, and compromise to facilitate resolution and restore harmony in the team.

Seek Mediation if Necessary: If conflicts persist or escalate, seek mediation or intervention from a neutral third party to facilitate resolution. Engage HR professionals, team leads, or external mediators to help facilitate difficult conversations and mediate disputes impartially. Provide a safe and confidential space for team members to express their concerns and work towards resolution with support from a mediator.

Document Agreements and Decisions: Document agreements, decisions, and resolutions reached during conflict resolution processes to ensure clarity and accountability. Keep records of discussions, action plans, and outcomes to prevent misunderstandings or disputes from arising in the future. Share documentation with relevant team members to ensure everyone is aligned and informed about the resolution.

Learn from Conflicts: Use conflicts and misunderstandings as opportunities for learning and growth within the remote team. Encourage team members to reflect on the root causes of conflicts, identify areas for improvement in communication and collaboration, and implement preventive measures to avoid similar issues in the future. Emphasize the importance of continuous improvement and adaptation in remote work environments.

Build Trust and Team Cohesion: Foster trust and team cohesion within the remote team to prevent conflicts and misunderstandings from arising. Invest in team-building activities, virtual social events, and opportunities for bonding to strengthen relationships and build rapport among team members. Encourage collaboration, recognition, and appreciation to cultivate a positive and supportive team culture.

CHAPTER 7

ADVANCING YOUR REMOTE CAREER

Remote work offers a wealth of opportunities for professional growth and advancement, allowing individuals to pursue fulfilling careers from anywhere in the world. Whether you're just starting your remote work journey or seeking to take your career to the next level, there are several strategies you can employ to advance your remote career:

Continuous Learning and Skill Development: Invest in continuous learning and skill development to stay competitive in the remote job market and expand your career opportunities. Take advantage of online courses, webinars, workshops, and certification programs to acquire new skills, deepen your expertise, and stay up-to-date with industry trends and best practices. Develop a growth mindset and embrace lifelong learning as a cornerstone of your remote career advancement.

Networking and Building Relationships: Cultivate a strong professional network and build meaningful relationships with peers, mentors, and industry professionals to advance your remote career. Attend virtual networking events, join professional organizations or online communities, and engage in networking activities to expand your network and connect with individuals who can provide guidance, support, and opportunities for career advancement.

Seek Growth Opportunities: Be proactive in seeking out growth opportunities within your current role or organization to advance your remote career. Volunteer for challenging projects, take on additional responsibilities, or seek opportunities for cross-functional collaboration to demonstrate your skills and potential for advancement. Communicate your career aspirations and goals to your employer and explore opportunities for career development, promotions, or advancement within the organization.

Build a Strong Personal Brand:
Establishing a strong personal brand is essential for standing out in the remote job market and advancing your career. Develop a professional online presence through platforms such as LinkedIn, personal websites, or professional portfolios to showcase your skills, expertise, and achievements. Craft a compelling personal brand narrative that highlights your unique value proposition and positions you as a sought-after remote professional in your field.

Set Clear Career Goals: Define
clear career goals and objectives for your remote career advancement and develop a strategic plan to achieve them. Identify short-term and long-term career goals, such as acquiring new skills, earning certifications, advancing to leadership roles, or transitioning to a new industry or specialization. Break down your goals into actionable steps and timelines, and regularly assess your progress and adjust your strategy as needed to stay on track towards achieving your career objectives.

Seek Feedback and Mentorship:
Solicit feedback from colleagues, supervisors, and mentors to gain insights into areas for improvement and growth in your remote career. Actively seek out mentorship relationships with experienced professionals who can provide guidance, advice, and support in navigating your remote career path. Be receptive to constructive feedback and use it as an opportunity for learning and development to enhance your skills and capabilities.

Demonstrate Leadership and Initiative:
Take initiative and demonstrate leadership qualities in your remote work environment to position yourself for career advancement. Lead by example, take ownership of projects, and inspire others through your actions and accomplishments. Identify opportunities to innovate, problem-solve, and drive positive change within your team or organization, and showcase your leadership potential to stakeholders and decision-makers.

Stay Flexible and Adaptive:
Remote work environments are constantly evolving, so it's essential to stay flexible

132

and adaptive in your approach to career advancement. Embrace change, adapt to new technologies and trends, and be willing to explore new opportunities and challenges that arise in the remote job market. Cultivate resilience, agility, and adaptability as essential skills for navigating the dynamic landscape of remote work and advancing your career successfully.

Seeking Opportunities for Growth and Advancement

In the realm of remote work, opportunities for growth and advancement abound for those willing to seek them out. Whether you're new to remote work or looking to elevate your career to new heights, actively pursuing opportunities for growth and advancement is essential. Here are some strategies to help you seek and seize opportunities for growth in your remote career:

Embrace Lifelong Learning: In the rapidly evolving landscape of remote work, continuous learning is key to staying relevant and advancing your career. Take advantage of online courses, webinars, workshops, and industry conferences to expand your skills and knowledge. Cultivate a growth mindset and approach each new learning opportunity as a chance to enhance your expertise and unlock new career possibilities.

Set Clear Career Goals: Define your career aspirations and set clear, actionable goals to guide your professional development journey. Whether you're aiming for a promotion, seeking to transition into a new role, or looking to acquire specific skills, having clear goals will help you stay focused and motivated. Break down your goals into smaller milestones and create a roadmap for achieving them over time.

Seek Feedback and Mentorship: Actively seek feedback from colleagues, supervisors, and mentors to gain insights into your strengths and areas for improvement. Constructive feedback can help you identify blind spots and areas where you can grow professionally. Establish mentorship relationships with experienced professionals who can provide guidance,

134

support, and advice as you navigate your remote career path.

Expand Your Network: Networking is a powerful tool for uncovering new opportunities and advancing your career in remote work. Join online communities, professional organizations, and industry groups relevant to your field to expand your network. Attend virtual networking events, engage in online discussions, and connect with professionals who share your interests and goals. Building a strong network can open doors to new opportunities, collaborations, and career advancement.

Volunteer for Challenging Projects: Volunteering for challenging projects is a proactive way to demonstrate your skills, initiative, and potential for growth within your organization or industry. Look for opportunities to take on new responsibilities, lead initiatives, or contribute to high-impact projects that align with your career goals. By stepping outside your comfort zone and tackling new challenges, you can showcase your abilities and position yourself for future growth and advancement.

135

Stay Current with Industry Trends: Stay informed about emerging trends, technologies, and best practices in your industry to stay ahead of the curve and remain competitive in the remote job market. Subscribe to industry publications, follow thought leaders on social media, and participate in online forums and discussions to stay up-to-date with the latest developments. By staying current with industry trends, you can position yourself as a knowledgeable and valuable asset within your field.

Take Ownership of Your Career Development: Ultimately, your career growth and advancement are in your hands. Take ownership of your career development by proactively seeking out opportunities for learning, growth, and advancement. Be proactive in identifying areas for improvement, seeking out new challenges, and advocating for yourself within your organization. By taking control of your career path and actively pursuing opportunities for growth, you can chart a course toward success in remote work.

Building a Personal Brand as a Remote Worker

In the competitive landscape of remote work, establishing a strong personal brand is essential for standing out, attracting opportunities, and advancing your career. Your personal brand is how you present yourself to the world and what sets you apart from others in your field. Here are some strategies for building a compelling personal brand as a remote worker:

Define Your Unique Value Proposition:
Start by defining your unique value proposition - what sets you apart from others in your field and makes you valuable to employers or clients. Identify your strengths, skills, and expertise, and consider how you can leverage them to solve problems and add value in your industry. Your value proposition should be clear, concise, and compelling, highlighting what makes you uniquely qualified for remote work opportunities.

Craft Your Brand Narrative:
Develop a cohesive brand narrative that

137

tells your story and communicates your values, personality, and professional identity. Consider what you want to be known for and how you want to position yourself in the remote work landscape. Tell your story authentically, highlighting your background, experiences, and achievements in a way that resonates with your target audience and sets you apart from the competition.

Create a Professional Online Presence: Establishing a professional online presence is crucial for building your personal brand as a remote worker. Create a professional website or portfolio showcasing your work, skills, and accomplishments. Optimize your LinkedIn profile with a professional photo, compelling headline, and detailed summary highlighting your expertise and achievements. Use social media platforms strategically to share valuable content, engage with your audience, and showcase your expertise in your niche.

Demonstrate Thought Leadership: Position yourself as a thought leader in your industry by sharing

your knowledge, insights, and expertise with others. Write articles, blog posts, or whitepapers on topics relevant to your field and share them on your website, LinkedIn, or industry publications. Participate in online forums, webinars, or podcasts as a guest speaker or panelist to showcase your expertise and contribute to thought leadership discussions in your industry.

Build Your Network: Networking is essential for building your personal brand and expanding your professional opportunities in remote work. Connect with peers, mentors, influencers, and industry professionals in your niche to build relationships and foster collaborations. Attend virtual networking events, join professional groups or communities, and engage in online discussions to expand your network and establish meaningful connections with others in your field.

Seek Feedback and Testimonials: Solicit feedback and testimonials from clients, colleagues, and supervisors to validate your skills and credibility as a remote worker. Ask satisfied clients or collaborators to provide testimonials or endorsements highlighting your contributions and the value you bring to the table. Positive feedback and testimonials can enhance your credibility and reputation as a remote professional and help strengthen your personal brand.

Consistently Deliver Value:

Ultimately, your personal brand is built on the foundation of consistently delivering value and exceeding expectations in your work. Focus on delivering high-quality work, meeting deadlines, and exceeding client or employer expectations to build a reputation for excellence and reliability. Consistently delivering value will help you build trust, credibility, and goodwill with your audience and reinforce your personal brand as a remote worker.

Continuing Education and Professional Development

In the dynamic landscape of remote work, continuing education and professional development are essential for staying competitive, advancing your career, and thriving in your remote job. Whether you're seeking to expand your skill set, stay current with industry trends, or pursue new career opportunities, investing in ongoing learning and development is key. Here are some strategies for continuing education and professional development in remote work:

Online Courses and Certifications:

Take advantage of online courses, certifications, and training programs to enhance your skills and knowledge in your field. Platforms like Coursera, Udemy, and LinkedIn Learning offer a wide range of courses on topics ranging from technical skills to leadership development and personal growth. Invest in courses that align with your career goals and interests and provide opportunities for practical application in your remote job.

Webinars and Virtual Workshops:

Attend webinars, virtual workshops, and online conferences to stay current with industry trends, best practices, and emerging technologies. Many organizations and professional associations host virtual events that offer valuable insights, networking opportunities, and skill-building sessions. Look for events relevant to your field and participate actively to gain new knowledge, network with industry peers, and expand your professional network.

Professional Certifications and Credentials:
Earn professional certifications and credentials to demonstrate your expertise and credibility in your field. Research industry-specific certifications and credentials that are recognized and valued by employers in your industry. Whether it's a project management certification, a technical credential, or a specialized designation, obtaining professional certifications can enhance your qualifications and open doors to new career opportunities in remote work.

Networking and Mentorship:
Networking and mentorship are invaluable for professional development in remote work. Connect with peers, mentors, and industry professionals in your field to exchange ideas, share experiences, and gain insights into career advancement opportunities. Join online communities, professional associations, or networking groups for remote workers to expand your

network and cultivate relationships with others in your industry.

Skill-Based Learning Projects:

Engage in skill-based learning projects to apply and reinforce your knowledge and skills in real-world scenarios. Look for opportunities to participate in side projects, freelance gigs, or volunteer work that allow you to practice and develop your skills in a practical setting. Taking on challenging projects outside of your regular job can help you build your portfolio, gain valuable experience, and demonstrate your capabilities to potential employers or clients.

Continuous Feedback and Reflection:

Seek feedback from colleagues, supervisors, and mentors to identify areas for improvement and growth in your remote work. Actively solicit feedback on your performance, skills, and competencies, and use it as an opportunity for learning and development. Reflect on your experiences, successes, and challenges in remote work, and identify areas where you can continue to grow and evolve professionally.

Stay Current with Industry Trends: Stay informed about industry trends, advancements, and innovations to remain relevant and competitive in remote work. Subscribe to industry publications, follow thought leaders on social media, and participate in online forums and discussions to stay up-to-date with the latest developments in your field. Stay curious, explore new ideas, and embrace lifelong learning as a fundamental aspect of your professional development journey in remote work.

CHAPTER 8

SUCCESS STORIES AND CASE STUDIES

In "Remote Work: The Ultimate Guide to Finding Legitimate Work-From-Home Jobs," success stories and case studies serve as powerful illustrations of how individuals have successfully navigated the remote work landscape and achieved their career goals. These stories provide inspiration, insights, and practical advice for readers embarking on their own remote work journey. Here are a few examples of success stories and case studies that highlight the diverse opportunities and experiences in remote work:

From Corporate Cubicle to Remote Entrepreneur:

Meet Sarah, a former corporate professional who transitioned from the confines of the traditional office to the freedom of remote entrepreneurship. Through dedication, perseverance, and strategic planning, Sarah built a successful freelance business from home, offering marketing consulting

145

services to clients around the globe. Her story illustrates how remote work can provide opportunities for autonomy, flexibility, and professional fulfillment outside the confines of the traditional 9-to-5.

Finding Work-Life Balance Through Remote Work: Follow the journey of Mark, a busy parent who struggled to balance his career with his family responsibilities. By embracing remote work opportunities, Mark was able to reclaim his time and prioritize his family while continuing to excel in his career. Through remote work, Mark found the flexibility to create a schedule that allowed him to be present for his family while pursuing his professional goals, demonstrating the transformative power of remote work in achieving work-life balance.

Remote Work in Rural Communities: Explore the story of Emily, a resident of a rural community who leveraged remote work opportunities to overcome geographical barriers and access meaningful employment

opportunities. Despite living in a remote area with limited job prospects, Emily found remote work opportunities that allowed her to pursue her career goals without having to relocate. Her story highlights how remote work can create economic opportunities and bridge the gap between urban and rural communities.

Scaling a Remote Team for Global Impact:
Dive into the case study of TechCo, a tech startup that successfully scaled its remote team to drive global impact and innovation. By embracing remote work practices, TechCo was able to tap into a global talent pool, foster diversity and inclusion, and create a collaborative work culture that transcended geographical boundaries. Their experience showcases how remote work can enable companies to thrive in a rapidly changing digital landscape while attracting top talent from around the world.

Transitioning to Remote Work Amidst a Pandemic:
Hear from Laura, who found herself suddenly thrust into remote work due to the COVID-19 pandemic. Despite initial challenges and

147

uncertainties, Laura embraced remote work as an opportunity for personal and professional growth. Through resilience, adaptability, and perseverance, Laura successfully navigated the transition to remote work, discovering newfound flexibility, productivity, and work-life balance along the way. Her story reflects the resilience and agility required to thrive in remote work environments, even amidst unprecedented challenges.

Interview with Successful Remote Worker Emily Smith

Q: Can you tell us a bit about yourself and your remote work journey?

Emily: Sure! I'm Emily Smith, and I've been working remotely for the past five years. Before transitioning to remote work, I was feeling stuck in my career and frustrated with the lack of opportunities in my small town. I decided to explore remote work as a way to expand my horizons and access more meaningful job opportunities without having to relocate.

Q: What inspired you to pursue remote work?

Emily: Living in a rural community, I was limited by the job market in my area and felt like I was missing out on career advancement opportunities. Remote work seemed like the perfect solution to bridge the gap between my geographical location and my career aspirations. I was inspired by the idea of being able to work from anywhere and access a global talent pool without having to leave my hometown.

Q: What challenges did you encounter during your transition to remote work?

Emily: One of the biggest challenges I faced was adjusting to the remote work lifestyle and finding a work-life balance. Without the structure of a traditional office environment, it took some time to establish routines and boundaries to separate my work life from my personal life. Additionally, there were technical challenges related to setting up a home office and ensuring reliable internet connectivity in a rural area.

Q: How did you overcome these challenges?

Emily: Overcoming these challenges required a combination of patience, experimentation, and adaptation. I made a conscious effort to establish a dedicated workspace in my home and set boundaries to create a distinction between work time and personal time. I also invested in upgrading my internet connection and exploring alternative solutions to ensure reliable connectivity. It took time to find the right balance, but with persistence and determination, I was able to overcome these challenges and thrive in my remote work environment.

Q: What advice would you give to others aspiring to pursue remote work?

Emily: My advice to others considering remote work is to embrace the opportunity wholeheartedly and be prepared to adapt to new ways of working. Remote work offers incredible flexibility and freedom, but it also requires discipline, organization, and self-motivation. Take the time to set up a productive home office, establish routines that work for you, and communicate effectively with your colleagues and clients. Most importantly, don't be afraid to step outside your comfort zone and seize opportunities for growth and advancement in your remote career.

Q: What has been the most rewarding aspect of remote work for you?

Emily: The most rewarding aspect of remote work for me has been the ability to pursue my career goals without sacrificing my quality of life. Remote work has allowed me to live and work on my own terms, while still accessing meaningful job opportunities and contributing to impactful projects. I've been able to achieve a better work-life balance, spend more time with my family, and pursue personal interests outside of work. Overall, remote work has been a game-changer for me, and I'm grateful for the opportunities it has provided.

Real-life Examples of Remote Work Setups and Experiences

The Freelancer: Sarah is a freelance graphic designer who works remotely from her home office. She has set up a dedicated workspace in a spare room, complete with a comfortable desk, ergonomic chair, and dual monitors for increased productivity. Sarah enjoys the flexibility of remote work, allowing her to balance her creative projects with personal hobbies like painting and gardening. She collaborates with clients and colleagues virtually, using communication tools like Slack and Zoom to stay connected and deliver high-quality work on time.

The Digital Nomad: James is a digital nomad who travels the world while working remotely as a software developer. He embraces the nomadic lifestyle, moving from one destination to another every few months and exploring new cultures and experiences along the way. James relies on a lightweight laptop and a reliable internet connection to stay connected to his remote team and clients. He enjoys the freedom and adventure of remote work, balancing his professional responsibilities with outdoor adventures like hiking, surfing, and photography.

The Stay-at-Home Parent:

Maria is a stay-at-home parent who works remotely as a virtual assistant. She juggles her remote job with caring for her two young children, creating a flexible schedule that allows her to work during nap times and after bedtime. Maria has set up a mobile office in her living room, equipped with a laptop, wireless headset, and a cozy corner for focused work sessions. She values the ability to earn an income while staying home with her children and appreciates the support of her remote team and clients.

The Remote Team Leader:

Alex is a remote team leader who oversees a distributed team of developers working from different time zones. He embraces asynchronous communication and flexible work hours to accommodate his team's diverse schedules and preferences. Alex relies on project management tools like Trello and Asana to track progress, assign tasks, and collaborate effectively with his remote team. Despite the challenges of managing a remote team, Alex values the autonomy and trust that remote work fosters, empowering his team members to thrive in their roles.

The Remote Intern: Emma is a college student who landed a remote internship with a marketing agency. She works remotely from her dorm room, attending virtual meetings, and collaborating with her team on marketing campaigns and social media projects. Emma appreciates the opportunity to gain real-world experience and build her professional network while balancing her academic studies. She relies on time management tools like Todoist and Google Calendar to stay organized and meet deadlines in her remote internship.

Lessons Learned and Key Takeaways

Throughout "Remote Work: The Ultimate Guide to Finding Legitimate Work-From-Home Jobs," readers have been exposed to a wealth of information, insights, and real-life examples aimed at guiding them through the remote work landscape. Here are some key lessons learned and takeaways from the book:

Flexibility and Adaptability:

Remote work offers unparalleled flexibility, allowing individuals to create their own schedules and work environments. However, adapting to remote work requires discipline, organization, and effective time management skills.

Embracing Technology:

Technology plays a crucial role in remote work, enabling communication, collaboration, and productivity. Embrace tools and platforms that facilitate remote work, such as video conferencing software, project management tools, and communication apps.

Clear Communication:

Effective communication is essential for remote work success. Be proactive in communicating with colleagues, supervisors, and clients, and establish clear expectations regarding communication channels, response times, and availability.

Building a Personal Brand:
Establishing a strong personal brand is critical for standing out in the remote job market. Craft a compelling online presence, showcase your skills and expertise, and network with industry professionals to enhance your visibility and credibility.

Continuous Learning and Development:
Remote work presents opportunities for continuous learning and professional development. Invest in expanding your skill set, staying current with industry trends, and seeking out growth opportunities to advance your remote career.

Work-Life Balance:
Maintaining a healthy work-life balance is essential for remote workers' well-being and productivity. Set boundaries between work and personal life, prioritize self-care, and create routines that promote balance and fulfillment.

Overcoming Challenges:
Remote work comes with its own set of challenges, such as isolation, distractions, and

technological issues. Learn to overcome these challenges by staying adaptable, seeking support when needed, and implementing strategies to mitigate common pitfalls.

Networking and Collaboration:
Building relationships and collaborating with others is key to success in remote work. Network with peers, mentors, and industry professionals, and leverage collaboration tools and platforms to foster connections and teamwork.

Resilience and Perseverance:
Remote work requires resilience and perseverance in the face of setbacks and obstacles. Stay resilient, embrace a growth mindset, and view challenges as opportunities for learning and growth.

Celebrating Successes: Finally,
celebrate your successes and milestones along the remote work journey. Recognize your achievements, acknowledge your progress, and take pride in the impact you're making as a remote worker.

CHAPTER 9

CONCLUSION

"Remote Work: The Ultimate Guide to Finding Legitimate Work-From-Home Jobs" has been a comprehensive journey through the world of remote work, offering valuable insights, practical advice, and real-life examples to empower readers in their pursuit of legitimate remote job opportunities. As we come to the conclusion of this guide, let's reflect on the key themes and takeaways that have emerged throughout our exploration of remote work.

Remote work has emerged as a transformative force in the modern workforce, offering unprecedented flexibility, autonomy, and opportunities for professionals to pursue meaningful careers from anywhere in the world. From corporate professionals seeking a better work-life balance to entrepreneurs building successful businesses from their homes, remote work has opened doors to new possibilities and redefined the traditional notions of work and productivity.

158

Throughout this guide, we've explored the importance and prevalence of remote work, delved into the skills and traits required for success in remote roles, and provided practical strategies for finding legitimate remote job opportunities. We've discussed the advantages and benefits of remote work, as well as the challenges and misconceptions that remote workers may encounter along the way.

We've heard inspiring success stories and learned valuable lessons from experienced remote workers, gaining insights into the diverse experiences and opportunities that remote work offers. From setting boundaries and managing time effectively to building a personal brand and fostering communication in remote teams, we've covered a wide range of topics aimed at helping readers navigate the remote work landscape with confidence and success.

As we conclude our exploration of remote work, it's important to remember that remote work is not just a trend or a temporary solution it's a fundamental shift in the way we work and live. Whether you're a seasoned remote professional or just beginning your remote work journey, the principles and strategies outlined in this guide will serve as valuable tools for navigating the ever-evolving world of remote work.

In closing, I encourage you to embrace the opportunities, challenges, and possibilities that remote work presents. Stay curious, stay adaptable, and stay connected with your fellow remote professionals as you embark on your own remote work journey. With determination, resilience, and a commitment to continuous learning and growth, you'll find success and fulfillment in the world of remote work.

Recap of Key Points

Throughout "Remote Work: The Ultimate Guide to Finding Legitimate Work-From-Home Jobs," we've explored a comprehensive roadmap to navigating the remote work landscape and finding legitimate remote job opportunities. Here's a recap of the key points covered in the book:

Understanding Remote Work: We

began by defining remote work and exploring its importance and prevalence in today's digital age. Remote work offers flexibility, autonomy, and opportunities for professional growth, making it an attractive option for many individuals.

Benefits and Advantages: We
discussed the advantages of remote work, including flexibility, work-life balance, cost savings, and access to global job opportunities. Remote work offers numerous benefits for both employers and employees, fostering productivity, creativity, and collaboration.

Challenges and Misconceptions:
Despite its benefits, remote work also presents challenges such as isolation, distractions, and communication barriers. We debunked common misconceptions about remote work and discussed strategies for overcoming challenges and maximizing success in a remote work environment.

Skills and Traits for Success:
Successful remote workers possess a unique set of skills and traits, including self-discipline, communication skills, adaptability, and time management. We explored these essential skills and

discussed strategies for developing and honing them for remote work success.

Finding Legitimate Remote Jobs: We provided a comprehensive guide to finding legitimate remote job opportunities, including researching job boards and platforms, networking, and avoiding scams and red flags. We discussed effective strategies for crafting compelling job applications and standing out in the remote job market.

Navigating Remote Work Platforms: We explored popular remote work platforms and discussed how to create appealing profiles, understand platform etiquette, and maximize success on these platforms. We also provided an overview of real-life examples of remote work setups and experiences.

Professional Development and Growth: Continuous learning and professional development are essential for success in remote work. We discussed strategies for advancing your skills, staying current with industry trends, and seizing

opportunities for growth and advancement in remote work.

Maintaining Work-Life Balance:

Finally, we emphasized the importance of maintaining work-life balance in remote work. We discussed strategies for setting boundaries, managing stress and burnout, and prioritizing self-care to ensure overall well-being and success in remote work.

Final Thoughts on the Future of Remote Work

As we conclude "Remote Work: The Ultimate Guide to Finding Legitimate Work-From-Home Jobs," it's essential to reflect on the future of remote work and its implications for individuals, businesses, and society as a whole. Remote work has experienced unprecedented growth and adoption in recent years, driven by technological advancements, changing attitudes towards work, and global events such as the COVID-19 pandemic. Looking ahead, the future of remote work holds immense potential and opportunities for individuals and organizations alike.

Continued Growth and Adoption:
Remote work is here to stay, with a growing number of companies embracing flexible work arrangements and remote-friendly policies. As technology continues to advance and remote work becomes more mainstream, we can expect to see further growth and adoption of remote work across industries and sectors.

Global Talent Pool:
Remote work has democratized access to job opportunities, allowing individuals to work from anywhere and access a global talent pool. Businesses can tap into diverse talent from around the world, fostering innovation, creativity, and collaboration on a global scale.

Redefining Work-Life Balance:
Remote work has challenged traditional notions of work-life balance, allowing individuals to design their own schedules and prioritize their well-being. As remote work becomes more prevalent, we can expect to see a shift towards a more flexible and holistic approach to work, with a greater emphasis on employee well-being and fulfillment.

Impact on Urbanization and Economic Development:

Remote work has the potential to reshape urbanization patterns and economic development, as individuals have the freedom to live and work in locations of their choosing. This decentralization of work can lead to revitalization of rural communities, reduced congestion in urban centers, and increased economic opportunities for regions outside of major metropolitan areas.

Challenges and Opportunities:

While remote work offers numerous benefits, it also presents challenges such as isolation, communication barriers, and technological issues. As remote work continues to evolve, it will be essential for individuals and organizations to address these challenges and seize opportunities for growth and innovation.

Embracing Change and Adaptation:

The future of remote work will be characterized by change, innovation, and adaptation. Individuals and organizations must embrace a growth mindset, stay agile and adaptable, and

165

continuously evolve to meet the evolving needs and demands of the remote work landscape.

Encouragement and Resources for Readers Embarking on Their Remote Work Journey

Embarking on a remote work journey can be both exciting and daunting. As you navigate the remote work landscape, remember that you're not alone. Countless individuals have successfully transitioned to remote work and found fulfillment and success in their careers. Here are some words of encouragement and resources to support you on your remote work journey:

Believe in Yourself: Believe in your abilities and trust that you have what it takes to succeed in remote work. Embrace new challenges with confidence and approach them with a positive mindset. Remember that every step you take towards your remote work goals is a step closer to realizing your dreams.

Stay Resilient: Remote work comes with its own set of challenges, but resilience is key to overcoming obstacles and thriving in a remote work environment. Stay resilient in the face of setbacks, adapt to change, and view challenges as opportunities for growth and learning.

Seek Support: Don't hesitate to seek support from friends, family, and colleagues as you navigate your remote work journey. Surround yourself with a supportive network of individuals who believe in your potential and can offer guidance, encouragement, and advice along the way.

Continuously Learn and Grow: Embrace a mindset of continuous learning and growth as you embark on your remote work journey. Invest in expanding your skill set, staying current with industry trends, and seeking out opportunities for professional development and advancement.

Explore Remote Work Resources: Take advantage of the wealth of resources available to remote workers, including online courses, webinars, podcasts, and networking events. Explore remote work platforms, job boards, and communities to connect with like-minded individuals and access valuable insights and opportunities.

Prioritize Work-Life Balance:
Maintain a healthy work-life balance by setting boundaries, prioritizing self-care, and creating routines that support your well-being. Remember that your health and happiness are essential to your success in remote work.

Celebrate Your Progress: Celebrate
your achievements and milestones along the remote work journey, no matter how small they may seem. Recognize your progress, acknowledge your growth, and take pride in the steps you're taking towards building the career and life you desire.

Remember that remote work is not just about finding a job; it's about crafting a lifestyle that aligns with your values, goals, and aspirations. Embrace the opportunities, challenges, and adventures that come with remote work, and trust that your journey will lead you to new horizons and exciting possibilities. You have the power to shape your own remote work destiny seize it with enthusiasm, determination, and a sense of adventure.

www.ingramcontent.com/pod-product-compliance
Lightning Source LLC
Chambersburg PA
CBHW071249050326
40690CB00011B/2318